# Cotswold W

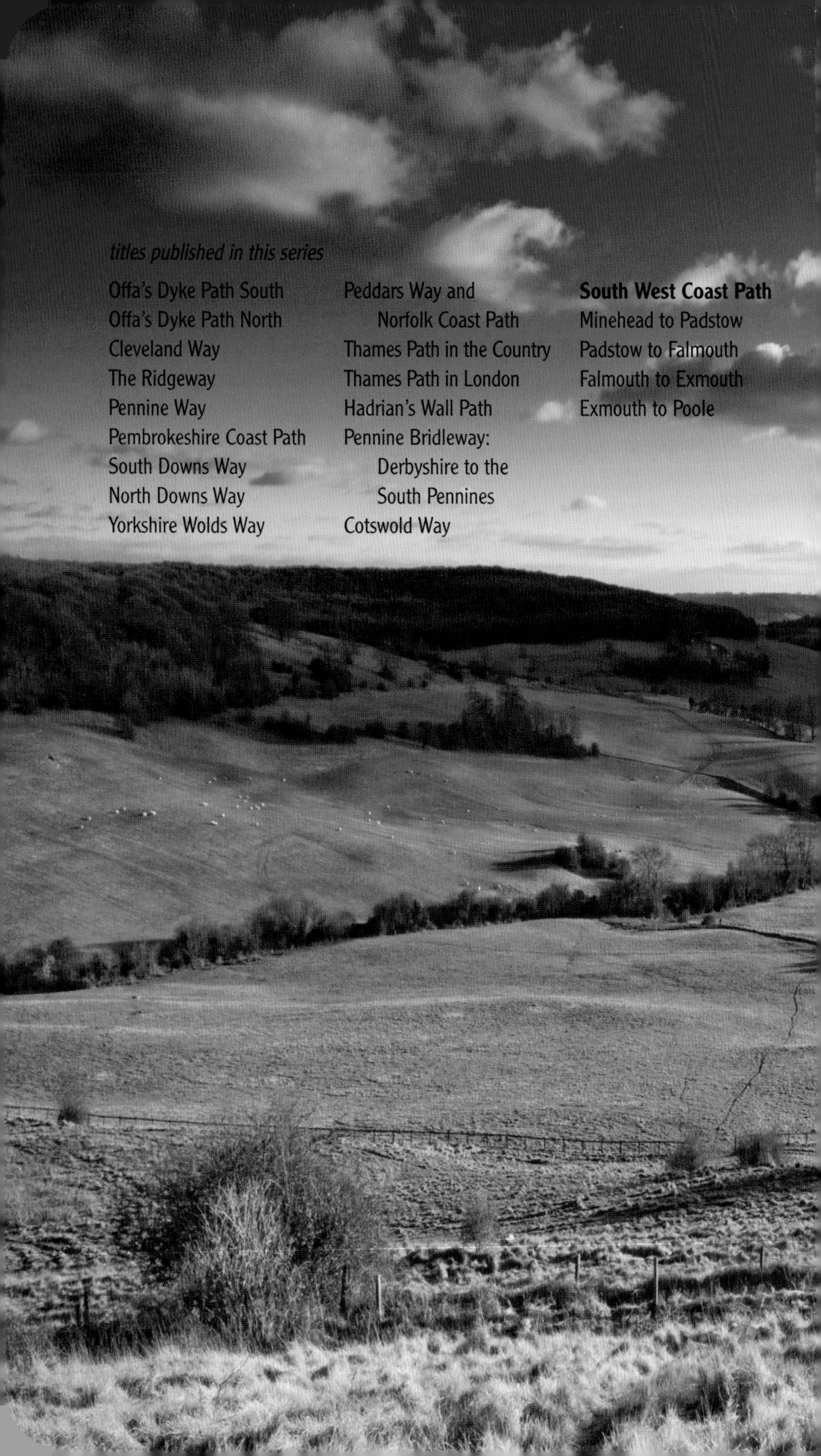

*titles published in this series*

Offa's Dyke Path South
Offa's Dyke Path North
Cleveland Way
The Ridgeway
Pennine Way
Pembrokeshire Coast Path
South Downs Way
North Downs Way
Yorkshire Wolds Way

Peddars Way and Norfolk Coast Path
Thames Path in the Country
Thames Path in London
Hadrian's Wall Path
Pennine Bridleway: Derbyshire to the South Pennines
Cotswold Way

**South West Coast Path**
Minehead to Padstow
Padstow to Falmouth
Falmouth to Exmouth
Exmouth to Poole

# Cotswold Way

Anthony Burton

Aurum

in association with

NATURAL ENGLAND

This fully revised and updated edition published in 2012 by Aurum Press Ltd
7 Greenland Street, London NW1 0ND
in association with Natural England.
www.naturalengland.org.uk
www.nationaltrail.co.uk
First published in 2003



A catalogue record for this book is available from the British Library.

ISBN 978 1 84513 785 4

Book design by Robert Updegraff
Printed and bound in China

Cover photograph: *Almshouses at Chipping Campden*
Half-title-page photograph: *Bath Abbey*
Title-page photograph: *The Cotswold escarpment*

Aurum Press want to ensure that these National Trail Guides are always as up to date as possible – but stiles collapse, pubs close and bus services change all the time. If, on walking this path, you discover any important changes of which future walkers need to be aware, do let us know. Either email us on **trailguides@aurumpress.co.uk** with your comments, or if you take the trouble to drop us a line to:

**Trail Guides, Aurum Press, 7 Greenland Street, London NW1 0ND,**

we'll send you a free guide of your choice as thanks.

# Contents

# How to use this guide

This guide is in three parts:

- The introduction, including historical background to the area and advice for walkers.
- The path itself, described in 15 chapters, with maps opposite each route description. This part of the guide also includes information on places of interest. Key sites are numbered in the text and on the maps to make it easy to follow the route description.
- The last part includes useful information such as how to get to the Trail, accommodation and organisations involved with the path.

The maps have been prepared by the Ordnance Survey for this guide using 1:25 000 maps as a base. The line of the Cotswold Way is shown in yellow, with the status of each section of the path – footpath or bridleway for example – shown in green underneath (see key on inside front cover). These rights-of-way markings also indicate the precise alignment of the path at the time of the original surveys, but in some cases the yellow line on these maps may show a route which is different from that shown by those older surveys, and in such cases walkers are recommended to follow the yellow route in this guide, which is waymarked with the distinctive acorn symbol used for all National Trails. Any parts of the path that may be difficult to follow on the ground are clearly highlighted in the route description, and important points to watch for are marked with letters in each chapter, both in the text and on the maps. *Some maps start on a right-hand page and continue on the left-hand page – black arrows (➞) at the edge of the maps indicate the start point.*

Should there have been a need to alter the route for any reason since publication of this guide, walkers are advised to follow the waymarks or signs which have been put up on site to indicate this. Such changes will also be found listed on the Cotswold Way website.

# Distance checklist

This list will help you in calculating the distances between places on the Cotswold Way, whether you are planning your overnight stays, or checking your progress.

| | *approx. distance from previous location location* | |
|---|---|---|
| | *miles* | *km* |
| Chipping Campden Market Hall | 0 | 0 |
| Broadway | 6.0 | 9.6 |
| Stanton | 4.3 | 6.9 |
| Stanway | 1.5 | 2.3 |
| Hailes Abbey | 4.0 | 6.4 |
| Winchcombe | 2.3 | 3.7 |
| Belas Knap | 2.1 | 3.3 |
| Cleeve Hill | 3.6 | 5.7 |
| Dowdeswell | 5.5 | 8.9 |
| Seven Springs | 2.7 | 4.4 |
| Leckhampton Hill | 2.0 | 3.2 |
| Crickley Hill | 3.1 | 5.0 |
| Birdlip | 2.5 | 4.0 |
| Cooper's Hill | 3.0 | 4.8 |
| Painswick | 5.7 | 9.1 |
| Haresfield Beacon | 2.5 | 4.1 |
| King's Stanley | 4.5 | 7.2 |
| Uley Bury (via Selsley Common) | 5.3 (7.0) | 8.5 (11.3) |
| Dursley | 2.7 | 4.3 |
| North Nibley (by short route) | 4.8 (2.3) | 7.7 (3.7) |
| Wotton-under-Edge | 2.5 | 4.1 |
| Alderley | 4.1 | 6.6 |
| Hawkesbury | 3.3 | 5.2 |
| Old Sodbury | 5.4 | 8.6 |
| Tormarton | 2.3 | 3.8 |
| Dyrham Park | 4.2 | 6.7 |
| Cold Ashton | 2.4 | 3.9 |
| Grenville Monument | 2.8 | 4.6 |
| Weston | 5.0 | 8.0 |
| Bath Abbey | 2.4 | 3.9 |

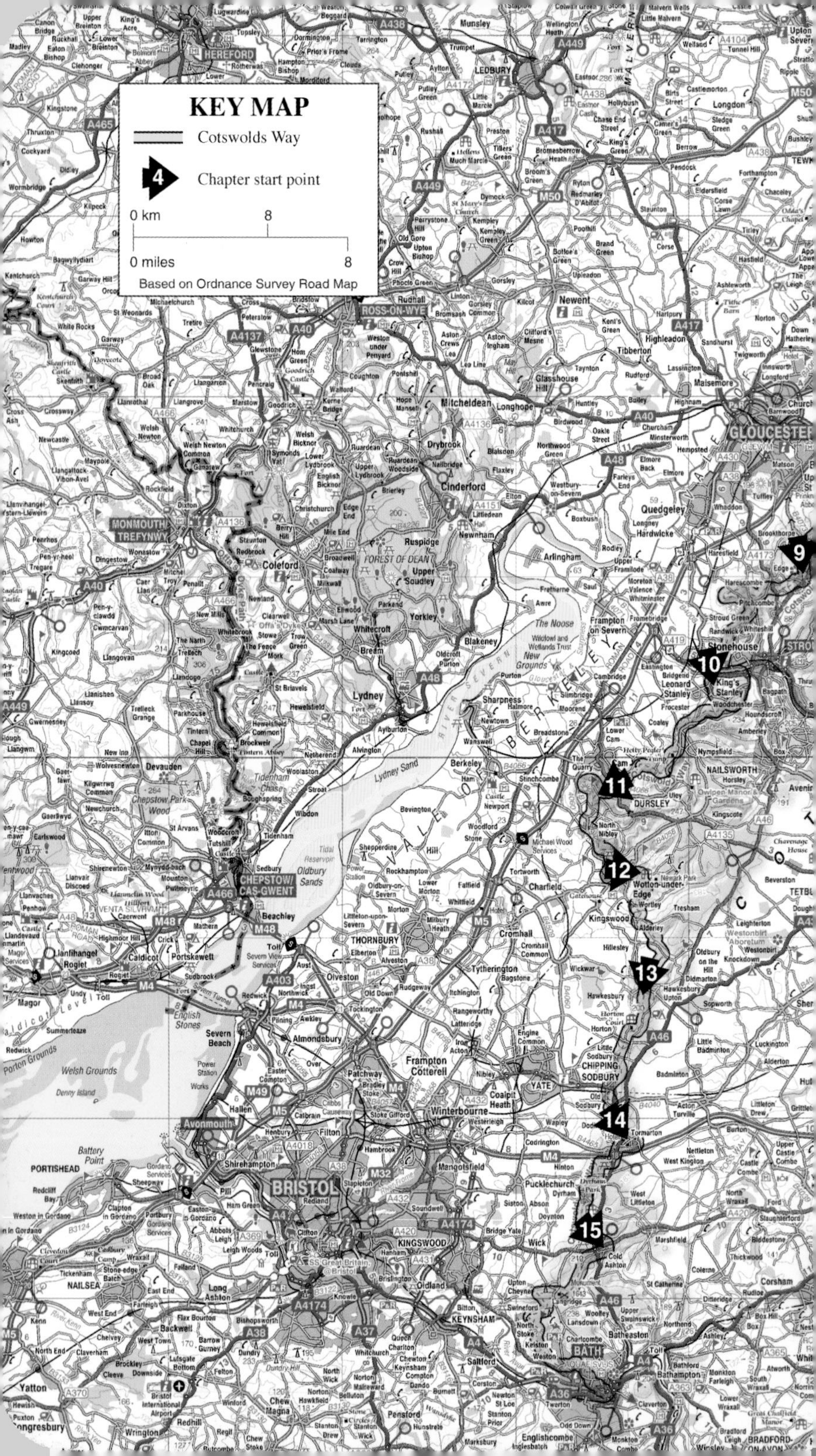

KEY MAP
Cotswolds Way
Chapter start point
0 km
8
0 miles
8
Based on Ordnance Survey Road Map
9
10
11
12
13
14
15

KEY MAP INDEX
1
2
3
4
5
6
7
8
CHELTENHAM
STOW-ON-THE-WOLD
CHIPPING NORTON
NORTHLEACH
BURFORD
Kington
Leominster
Worcester
Droitwich Spa
Redditch
Warwick
Daventry
Southam
Bromyard
Stratford-upon-Avon
Great Malvern
Pershore
Evesham
Malvern Hills
Hay-on-Wye
Hereford
Ledbury
Banbury
Brackley
Wye Valley
Moreton-in-Marsh
Tewkesbury
Stow-on-the-Wold
Chipping Norton
Ross-on-Wye
Crickhowell
Cheltenham
Abergavenny
Gloucester
The Cotswolds
Northleach
Kidlington
Monmouth
Burford
Oxford
Ebbw Vale
Witney
Lydney
Stroud
Lechlade on Thames
Usk
Pontypool
Cwmbran
Nailsworth
Cirencester
Chepstow
Abingdon
Tetbury
Cricklade
Faringdon
Malmesbury
Wantage
Didcot
Newport
Swindon
Yate
Avonmouth
CARDIFF
Chippenham
Clevedon
Bristol
Calne
Hungerford
Thatcham
Penarth
Marlborough
Weston-super-Mare
Bath
Melksham
Newbury
Devizes
North Wessex Downs
Pewsey
Trowbridge
Radstock
Cheddar
Burnham-on-Sea
Ludgershall
Basingstoke
Mendip Hills
Westbury
Frome
Warminster
Andover
Wells
Amesbury
Glastonbury
Shepton Mallet

# Preface

In 2007 the Cotswold Way became a National Trail. Following the limestone escarpment on the western edge of the Cotswolds, the 102-mile (164-km) route gives the walker a taste of a quintessentially English landscape that has been shaped by man's activities from prehistoric times.

The landscape that the Trail offers is as varied as it is beautiful: the bleakness and beauty of its highest section, Cleeve Common, contrasts with the gently rolling farmland and magnificent beech woodlands that characterise its central part, with their carpets of bluebells and wood anemone in the spring and their rich golden hues in the autumn. The stunning views over the Severn Vale, the Malvern Hills, the Forest of Dean, and even the Black Mountains in Wales on a clear day, will delight you from start to finish. It is the character of this landscape that brought about its designation as the Cotswolds Area of Outstanding Natural Beauty (AONB) in 1966 – now the largest area with this designation in England and Wales.

Throughout its length, from the market town of Chipping Campden in the north to the World Heritage city of Bath in the south, the Cotswold Way is steeped in history, passing Neolithic burial chambers, ancient hill forts, Bronze Age round barrows, Roman villas, historic houses, churches and abbeys.

The National Trail offers a unique opportunity to experience this area away from the hustle and bustle of the crowds and to travel at a leisurely pace. It can be enjoyed as a whole, or it can be walked in stages by devising a circular walk or using public transport – either way, this book is for you.

National Trails are the 'flagship' long-distance trails in England and Wales. They are funded by Natural England, working in partnership with local authorities and others to ensure they are maintained to the highest standards and are supported by excellent information to help you to plan your trip.

We will hope you will enjoy many delightful hours of walking through some of Britain's loveliest countryside.

# PART ONE
# Introduction

A peacock lords it over Newark Park.

*Typical Cotswold stone wall and a National Trail acorn marker post at the end of Mile Drive near Chipping Campden.*

# Walking the Cotswold Way

Why walk the Cotswold Way? One very good answer would be that you will be walking through the largest official Area of Outstanding Natural Beauty in Britain. To enjoy the experience to the full requires a certain amount of forward planning.

## Which direction?

The first decision that everyone setting out along the Way has to take is the direction in which to walk. There is no clear-cut 'better' route. There is a general rule that suggests that it is more sensible to walk north in Britain, and that would certainly apply to this area. The prevailing winds of the region are from the west to south-west, so that those following this route are likely to have the wind at their backs. They are also likely in wet weather to avoid the discomfort of rain in the face, while in fine weather they will have the advantage of not walking into the sun.

This guide, however, has been written as a description of the route from north to south. There is an argument that it is better to face a southerly breeze rather than a northerly gale, but that is not the reason for the choice in this case. It seems, somehow, perverse to begin the Cotswold Way with a complex walk up city streets: even if the city is a World Heritage site, it does not feel like the Cotswolds. Chipping Campden, by contrast, offers a start which could not be more Cotswoldian. Another factor which influenced the decision was accessibility. Transport to Chipping Campden is more difficult to organise than transport to Bath, the nearest railway station being at Moreton-in-Marsh, and buses are infrequent. While it is usually possible to make arrangements for getting to a starting point at a specific time, the end of a walk is more difficult to predict so that it is all too easy to miss the last, and possibly only, bus. Bath is well served by bus and train, and one can therefore be fairly certain of getting away with ease at any time. Finally, there is something to be said for ending a long walk in style, with a sense of triumph and achievement – and this is something Bath most certainly provides. The final section takes the walker past some of the most elegant Georgian architecture to be found anywhere and ends with the glories of the Abbey. These are sites which attract visitors from around the world, but somehow there is an extra satisfaction to be had from the knowledge that you haven't been cosseted in a coach but have tramped over a hundred miles to see them.

## Doing it in stages

The success of a long-distance walk often depends on the care taken in the planning and preparation. Not everyone, however, will want to start at one end and continue relentlessly to the other. Many will want to spread the walk over a long period of time, doing perhaps no more than a few miles in a day and returning for more at a later date. The directions in this book are equally suitable for all users.

## How long will it take?

The route has been divided into what should be manageable sections for those who only want to do parts of the route, or want to do the whole walk in easy stages and to do so at a leisurely pace. Others will run sections together to make for a fuller day. Intermediate distances can be found in the Distance Checklist on page 7. The decision will depend, to some extent, on how far one can comfortably walk in a day. Do not underestimate the Cotswolds. This may not be a mountainous area, but there is no shortage of sharp climbs and awkward descents to slow the walker down, and it is better to arrive ahead of schedule, fresh and well, than to trudge on into the dusk, tired and miserable. It is amazing how much longer the last mile seems than the first. When it comes to pacing yourself, it is impossible to lay down rules, as individuals have different attitudes and different levels of fitness. For those who are really unsure about their capabilities, a useful starting point is Naismith's Rule. This states that a reasonable average is 2.5 miles (4 km) in an hour, but an extra 4 minutes needs to be added for every 100 feet (30 metres) climbed. For example, the walk from Stanway to Hailes Abbey is just 4 miles (6.5 km), so it should take slightly over an hour and a half, but there is a total climb of just over 550 feet (170 metres), which brings the total time up to 2 hours. Most walkers aiming to complete the whole distance in one trip find that allowing between seven and nine days from end to end makes for a comfortable and pleasant trip. Many, however, will want to allow longer, to pause and enjoy the interesting sites along the route.

## Equipment, maps and signage

Any long-distance walk is made more agreeable if one has the right equipment. Good walking boots are essential, on a route with no shortage of steep hills and rough ground. Good weatherproof clothing is equally necessary. The map might suggest that the whole route is little more than a gentle country stroll, but even in summer the wind can whistle over the exposed uplands, bringing cold, driving rain. Winters here can be hard, and with much of the land at over 1,000 feet (300 metres) walkers can be faced with snow even if the valleys are clear. Those who set out to do the entire walk in one go can only guess at what the weather might be when they reach the final stretch. This is not meant to be alarmist. The great majority of walkers will enjoy a trouble-free journey, but it is common sense to prepare for the worst likely conditions. If bad weather does not arrive, nothing is lost; if it does, then being ready for it can make the difference between pleasure and discomfort or worse.

The Cotswold Way existed for many years as a recreational footpath, but in its upgrading to a National Trail, many changes have been made. The most important of these involve changes in the actual route. One result of this is that the older Ordnance Survey maps will not show the new line. The route as mapped and described in this book incorporates all the changes and was accurate at the time of writing, but there are occasions when alterations have to be made, even if only temporarily, for example for necessary maintenance work. It is possible to

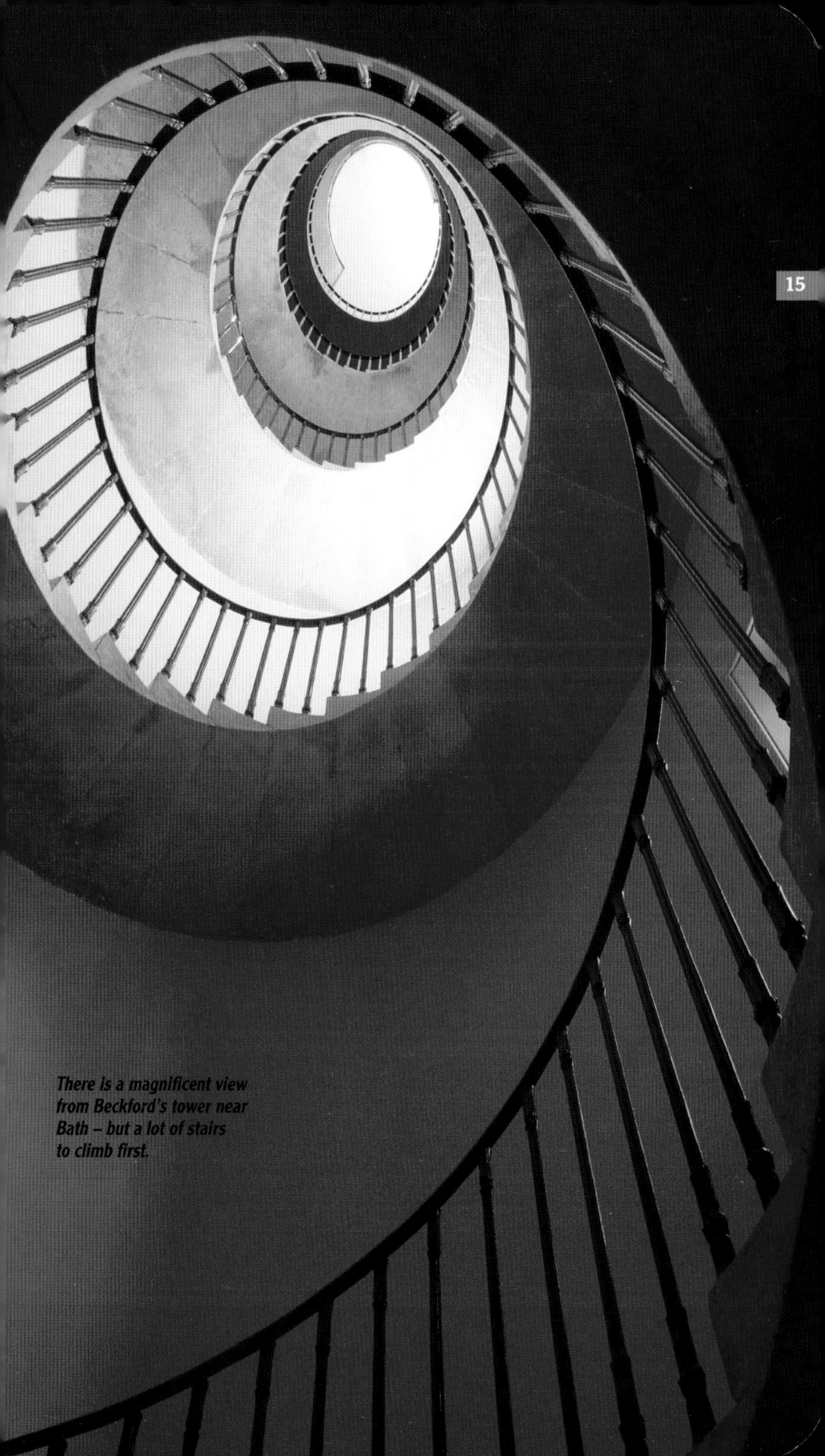

*There is a magnificent view from Beckford's tower near Bath – but a lot of stairs to climb first.*

*A mature beech spreads autumnal leaves over the path between Alderley and Lower Kilcott. These magnificent trees dominate the woodland along the Cotswold Way.*

check in advance, as the information is always available on the Cotswold Way National Trail website. If that happens, diversion notices will be posted, and these should always be followed. Walkers who know the old route will be delighted to find the improvements that have been made along the way, from clearer signposting and better footpath surfaces to safer road crossings, all designed to improve the experience of walking the Cotswold Way.

## Safety

All the normal rules of country walking apply in the Cotswolds: have your maps with you and a compass – and if you do not know how to use the latter, find out. This guide should enable you to find your way with little trouble, and waymarks are in place throughout the walk, carrying the acorn mark indicating that this is a National Trail. Many guidebooks discourage the solitary walker, but there is no reason why you

*Bath Abbey provides a magnificent finale to the Cotswold Way.*

should not walk on your own if you want to, providing you take elementary precautions. Tell someone where you are going and when you expect to arrive. Accidents can happen, and no one wants to be left stranded, hoping that perhaps they will be missed. Even in the age of the ubiquitous mobile phone, this is still a sensible strategy, as network coverage is not always available. In the end, it comes down to common sense. A walk along the Cotswold Way is not a Himalayan trek, but good planning and sensible precautions are as advisable for one as they are for the other. Take a little time to think ahead and you can be sure of enjoying a magnificent long-distance walk.

## Public transport and parking

Those who are doing the route end to end will find it most convenient to use public transport, and there is a lot to be said for using these services even when doing short sections. Some, however, will travel to the Trail by car and will want to park their cars in convenient places, close to the route. Where there are recommended parking places, they are listed at the start of each section. It is important to keep the goodwill of the locals by using these designated areas, rather than using up scarce spaces or blocking the way in towns and villages and on narrow country lanes. If no site is indicated, please make sure that you are not causing any sort of obstruction to others. Courtesy shown by walkers will help to ensure that others who follow on will be met with goodwill, not resentment.

## Accommodation

There are other things to take into consideration for the long-distance walker. Accommodation is not a real problem, but may involve a detour off the route. Hotels, guest houses and B&Bs are in plentiful supply along the Trail, but places to camp are few and far between, so campers may have to spend the occasional night in a B&B. In a popular area such as this accommodation may be quite heavily booked in holiday seasons. It is therefore a very good idea to work out each overnight stop in advance and make an early booking. An alternative is to make use of one of the agencies, which will book accommodation and even move your luggage for you. Food and drink are not always available without a detour, so it is as well to plan in advance to make sure that you have the food – and, more importantly, drink – that you need for the day. Details on how to get this information can be found at the end of the book. Far and away the best source for facts about all the facilities along the way is *The Cotswold Way National Trail Companion.*

## Respect the land

Although this is a walk that offers a sense of being in unspoilt open countryside for a great deal of the way, it is in fact a managed landscape and much of the land to either side of the Way is in private ownership. It is up to every walker to respect the rights of others who earn their living on this land and do not simply come here for recreation. Basically this means little more than following the Countryside Code, and being particularly aware of security for fields with livestock and taking care to keep to the designated right-of-way through woodland, pasture and arable land.

# The natural landscape

It is easy enough to recognise when one is in the Cotswolds: the gentle swell of the upland laced with drystone walls, the nestling villages of rich, creamy stone. It is a good deal more difficult to give precise boundaries to the region. To the east there is a steady, almost imperceptible rise out of the clays of Northamptonshire and Oxfordshire, so that to those who approach from this direction, the Cotswolds rarely seem like hills at all. There are no sudden dramatic rises, no stern craggy faces, and only rarely do the hills manage to creep over the 1,000-foot (300-metre) mark, generally settling for a more modest elevation. Stripped of earth and grass, the area would be revealed as a vast slab of rock, tilted up from east to west. The one really well-defined boundary comes on this western side, where the Cotswolds meet the Severn Vale, and the rock has eroded away to leave a steep escarpment. It is this escarpment that the Cotswold Way follows. But if the boundaries are difficult to set, the unifying factor is easily found in the underlying limestone. This can be seen as pale fragments in the fields or exposed along the escarpment edge; and it is also found in houses, barns and field walls. It is all pervasive.

The limestone of this region is predominantly oolitic. Seen under the microscope, the rock appears full of minute globules like fish roe, and it is from the Greek for 'egg stone' that its name derives. The 'roe' is in fact nothing more than a grain of sand, smoothly coated with calcium carbonate. It is the nature of this rock that gives character to the scenery, as it is worn away in smooth contours to produce the gentle curves in the landscape. Above it the soil is thin and stony and the upland is comparatively bare of trees. At one time it was still more so, for the area was largely given over to sheep grazing. In the 18th century, however, landlords dotted the countryside with copses, mainly composed of beech, which remains the dominant tree to this day. In contrast, the deep valleys scored through the plateau are often densely wooded and have a remote, almost mysterious character all their own. Some of these valleys are an enigma, for they no longer carry any trace of river or stream. It might appear that the streams have simply disappeared, having long since found an alternative route. But in fact these valleys were not created by streams at all, but by the meltwater from the thaw that brought an end to the last Ice Age.

The treeless upland has never been the most hospitable of areas, swept by the wind, regularly buried under winter snows, and with little in the way of a water supply to encourage settlement. Not surprisingly, it was along the spring line at the foot of the escarpment and in the valleys and hollows that villages and towns were begun and developed through the centuries. These factors combine to create the rich and varied landscape that makes the Cotswold Way such an enjoyable walk and a visual delight. This same variety also provides a number of very different habitats for plants and wildlife.

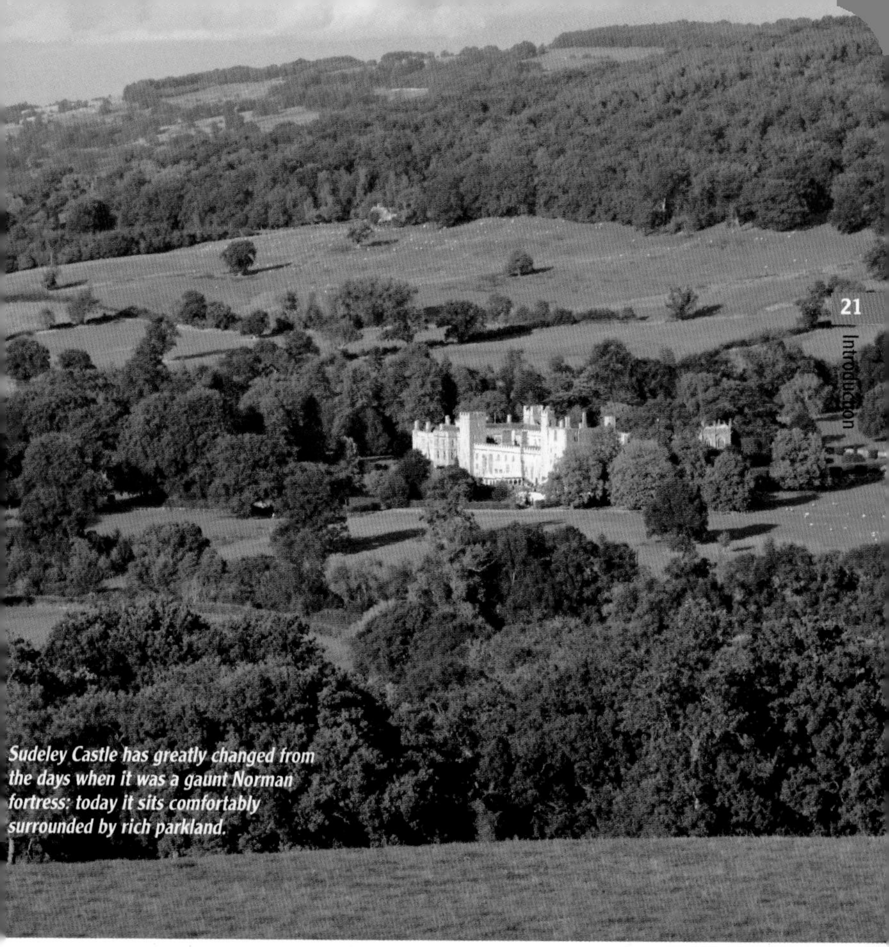
Sudeley Castle has greatly changed from the days when it was a gaunt Norman fortress: today it sits comfortably surrounded by rich parkland.

One of the great advantages of walking through a region, as opposed to driving or even cycling, is that it is always possible to pause, look and listen, and the Cotswold hills offer rich rewards for those prepared to take their time. It brings to mind these famous lines on the subject:

*What is this life if, full of care,*
*We have no time to stand and stare?*

It is not perhaps too surprising to find that W. H. Davies, the author of the poem, lived in the area. He settled in Nailsworth, and regularly walked over Selsley Common, which is crossed by the Cotswold Way. The Common itself represents just one type of environment that the walker will enjoy. As well as these grassy uplands, there are woods and farmland. Even urban areas offer their own wildlife interest, as the Cotswolds are well known for their cottage gardens, which attract a rich array of birds and insects.

Historically, cultivation of the uplands took second place to the more profitable activity of sheep grazing. The close-cropped sheep's fescue and red fescue thrived, but as the sheep became less common, taller grasses, such as tor grass, have been able to flourish and become dominant. Grass is such a ubiquitous ground cover that it is easy to overlook how varied the different grasses are, and how much they contribute to the landscape. Wild flowers are more obviously attractive, and there are some lovely examples to be found here, from the quite commonplace, but very beautiful, bird's-foot trefoil to the more exotic orchids, which come in a number of different varieties. Some areas are noted for particularly fine displays, such as Cleeve Hill, with its rich summer covering of harebells. The vetches are especially important, as they attract butterflies, kidney vetch being particularly favoured by the common blue, the chalkhill blue and fritillaries. Meadow brown have more modest tastes, preferring grasses, and cabbage white thrive despite the lack of cabbage. Birdlife is plentiful, but there is one species which is sure to be encountered: the meadow pipit. It is not perhaps one of the most exciting

*Wood anemone brighten the beechwoods in spring.*

birds to look at, but its song is a welcome accompaniment to any walk. It sounds rather feeble as it rises from the ground, but it produces a beautiful melody as it sinks back down again. It can easily be confused with the skylark. They look quite similar, though the skylark boasts a punk hairstyle, standing up in tufts on the top of its head, and it sings from high above the ground. The high ground is also the place to look for birds of prey, notably the buzzard and the kestrel.

Woodland offers a very different habitat. The Cotswold woods tend to change as they climb the escarpment slope. Lower down is scrub, sycamore and ash, but nearer the rim the beech dominates everything. These beechwood hangers are a glory at any time of the year, but reach their finest hour in autumn, when they burnish the hillsides with gold. At other times of the year, the flowers on the floor have their days of stardom. Spring is particularly fine, when the bluebells, wood anemone and dog's mercury are at their best. Summer brings the pungent aroma of wild garlic. Birds are trickier to spot among the close-packed trees, but they can always be heard. There is the rat-a-tat-tat of the woodpecker providing a rhythmic accompaniment to the sweet song of the chiffchaff.

Farmland offers its own delight. Summer fields of poppies, once so familiar, but now alas a rarity, are still to be found in the Cotswolds. Hedgerows are comparatively rare: this is the land of stone walls, but they too have their own interest. Lichens give them colour and flowers such as stone crop and herb Robert flourish. There is the usual selection of birds, but there is always the chance of seeing something a little different, such as a partridge. It is not, however, likely to be the native grey-leg partridge, but much more probably the imported red-leg. But as the red-leg has been with us for over three centuries, perhaps it should be granted honorary citizenship.

The area has its own specialities. The teasel is not an uncommon plant, but it has a special place in the history of the region. Teasels have been used in the woollen industry for centuries (see page 29), though not the common teasels. The cultivated fuller's teasel has hooked spikes, where the common teasel spikes are straight. And many of the plants have their own local names. The delightful early purple orchid has not come out very well in the process, known as dead-man's finger or bloody-man's finger and somewhat puzzlingly as goosey-gander. Bird's-foot trefoil is the bacon-and-egg plant or, more oddly, pattens and clogs. A personal favourite is the hawthorn – the hippety-haw tree, which seems to catch its frothy, white exuberance when in bloom.

Wild animals are rarely seen, with rabbits the most likely sighting, though the walker might share the author's experience of being joined by a nonchalant fox that appeared on the path ahead and wandered along, quite unconcerned by its human companion. Deer live in some of the woodland areas, but they are remarkably elusive. Whether plant, bird or animal, there will always be something to enjoy along the way.

*The Market Hall at Chipping Campden.*

## The historic landscape

The geology of the region has done more than anything else to determine man's place in the Cotswolds and how the resources have been used. Wealth was created in the uplands, based on the grazing sheep with their fine fleeces, but it was in the valleys that the money was spent. Here, villages were constructed of mellow stone, often enriched with churches of a grandeur that seems out of all proportion to the communities they serve. The Cotswold towns and villages represent for many the true English idyll, made all the more attractive by the contrast with the stark uplands. The region sometimes seems so perfect that it might all have been designed as a tourist-board advert. But it was not always so favourably viewed. The famous wit Sydney Smith travelled through the Cotswolds early in the 19th century and was not pleased at all with what he found:

'You travel for twenty or five-and-twenty miles over one of the most unfortunate desolate counties under heaven, divided by stone walls, and abandoned to the screaming kites and larcenous crows: after travelling really twenty and to

appearances ninety miles over this region of stone and sorrow, life begins to be a burden, and you wish to perish.'

He only cheered up when he reached the scarp edge at Birdlip and looked out over the lush Severn Vale. It has to be said, however, that Smith was not the greatest enthusiast for rural life. He wrote in 1838: 'I have no relish for the country; it is a kind of healthy grave.' Very few who walk the Cotswold Way will find themselves sharing his opinions, but all will experience the same delighted astonishment at the 'strikingly sublime' views that suddenly open up along the escarpment.

Today, much of the pleasure of walking in the Cotswolds comes from discovering a world in which nature and man are brought together in close harmony. A drystone wall stands above a ditch from which the stones themselves were dug. The walker will pass a quarry and glance at the exposed stone, and a few minutes later see the same stone used for the farmhouse at the end of the lane; likewise, the stone of the village is that on which the village stands. The builders had no idea they were creating 'beauty spots'. They used the material that was at hand because it was the sensible, practical thing to do. They built in an unfussy style, largely dictated by the materials they used. They built solidly and well, and time has done the rest. Roofs sag lazily under the weight of centuries; moss and lichen colour and soften what was once hard-edged stone. The charm is not something artificial, but is deep seated and rooted in time and place.

The Cotswold Way offers the walker some of the best of the region, and certainly the most dramatic scenery. It also provides an historical perspective and an extraordinary sense of continuity. The techniques employed more than 5,000 years ago, for example, by the people of the Neolithic Age to build drystone walls for their long barrows or burial chambers, were also used to create modern field boundaries. Down through the centuries, changes have left their mark, but seem never to have altered the fundamental character of the area. Even the Industrial Revolution, which transformed so much of Britain, was comfortably absorbed into the Cotswold tradition. It is possible to travel the region and come away unaware that there were once around 150 textile mills at work here. Perhaps this is a clue to the enjoyment to be found by those who walk the Cotswold Way. There is a sense of passing through a landscape that has never broken free of the mould formed many centuries ago. There are occasional interruptions: the M4 certainly comes as a shock to eye and ear. But such intrusions are rare. Sometimes the Cotswolds are described as a 'picture-postcard' area, as though found guilty of some unspecified crime against modernity. Yet the scenery never falls into smug prettiness; the landscape is robust and the villages sturdy, and to walk from one end of the region to the other is a rare delight. This is due, in no small measure, to the sense of coherence that has come from thousands of years of use of Cotswold limestone.

The builders of the Cotswold area were doubly blessed: the local stone has a rare beauty and is easily worked, being relatively soft when taken from the quarry. This encouraged the local masons to shape it into smooth-faced blocks for even the most modest buildings and to add rich decorative details to the grandest. The style that is now considered typical of the Cotswolds owes everything to the nature of the stone. Because this was so readily available, even cottages were given an ashlar façade, one in which the stone is dressed to create a smooth front. Again, instead of having to skimp on materials on the upper floors by using dormer windows let into the roof, the Cotswold builder would often extend the walls upwards into gables. The ease of carving is reflected in the tall, shaped chimneys, mullioned windows and, most characteristically, in the dripstone mouldings above the windows. These are the basic elements of the Cotswold house, but there are endless variations and elaborations. Shapely finials stand above gables, doorways are surrounded by elaborate mouldings and, in the grander houses, details such as coats of arms are added. But whatever the design, cottage and manor share in the same splendour that derives from the stone itself. The limestone seems not so much to reflect the light as to absorb and throw it back, enriched with a deep, golden glow. Above all, the use of local stone creates a resonance between the houses and the ground on which they stand. One could not imagine the traditional Cotswold house being at home in any other region.

Cotswold stone is not used only for the façades of buildings. Some types of limestone are fissile, i.e. capable of being split into layers. This is the origin of the material variously known as 'stone tiles' or, more often in this area, 'stone slates'. Such slates were used for roofing, and it is the combination of stone walls and stone roof which produces the finest buildings in the Cotswolds. Traditionally, the stones were quarried, then laid out in winter and watered every day. All that was needed to split them was a hard frost and a quick thaw. An ordinary modern roof is built up of tiles of uniform size and thickness, but to construct a Cotswold roof, stone slates had to be roughly graded in size, with the smallest placed nearest to the ridge and the largest at the eaves. The different sizes each had their own name, such as muffities, wiretts and tauts. There were no precise measurements and, as a result, no two Cotswold roofs are ever quite the same. A rare opportunity to see the underside of a stone roof is provided by the Market Hall at Chipping Campden. Here one can see the size and shape of the individual stone slates, and how they are fixed to the battens by wooden pegs. The Cotswold house needed to be sturdy to support its roof, which weighed around 1 ton per 100 square feet (1 tonne per 9 square metres). Yet the overall effect is one of great charm, and it would be a hard-hearted soul who did not respond to this poem in stone. The rest of this introduction will give a brief chronological survey of the region.

## The prehistoric Cotswolds

The history of man's involvement in the Cotswolds goes back over 6,000 years. Remains have been found dating back to the Neolithic or New Stone Age, which lasted from around 4000 to 2000 BC. There are traces of a settlement at Crickley Hill, but the Neolithic camp here was apparently abandoned then reinhabited around 700 BC, when the defences were greatly strengthened. To obtain a glimpse of the culture of our distant ancestors, one has to turn to the structures they built for the dead. Known as long barrows, these tombs are virtually identical to others found in south Wales, indicating how the early farming communities gradually made their way eastwards across the Severn to the Cotswolds and onward into what is now Oxfordshire. There are many examples of such tombs, and two of the finest are to be seen on the Cotswold Way: Belas Knap and Nympsfield long barrow. In both cases, the stone burial chambers were covered by huge grassy mounds. Belas Knap has an impressive forecourt with delicate stone walls that lead to a false entrance; the actual entrance to the tomb is in the side of the mound. These two sites were used for many burials – over 30 skeletons were unearthed at Belas Knap and there may originally have been more. One can only guess at the nature of the religion which made such elaborate burials necessary.

The Stone Age ended with the introduction of metals, and around 2000 BC saw the beginning of the Bronze Age. Burial mounds can again be found dating from this period, although this time they are round barrows. The best example on the Way is Barrow Wake near Crickley Hill. With the arrival of the Iron Age, around 500 BC, came a period of great activity, when many of our most visible monuments were constructed. Dramatic hill forts were built along the line of the Cotswold escarpment, which improved on the defences offered by the steep hillsides by excavating deep ditches and using the rock and soil to build high ramparts. There are several examples along the Way, of which the forts of Uley and Painswick are the best in terms of location, but Sodbury Camp is probably the most complete.

The Romans first arrived in Britain in about 50 BC, and within a short time their influence was felt in this region. Cirencester was known as Corinium Dobunnorum, the regional capital of the Dobunni, and by the 2nd century AD was the largest town in Britain. It stood at the heart of a network of roads: Fosse Way, Akeman Street and Ermin Way. It also became an artistic centre, famous for its mosaicists. The Romans clearly liked the region and settled here, establishing a number of rich villas. The word 'villa' today suggests a modest suburban house, but these were grand houses surrounded by extensive agricultural estates. There would be mosaic pavements in the main rooms, bath houses and a hypocaust or central-heating system. They were the stately homes of their day. The Way runs past Witcombe villa, but there are far grander examples in the Cotswolds at Chedworth and North Leigh. The museum at Cirencester has many outstanding Roman remains on display.

The Cotswold Way National Trail is only the latest of many paths, tracks and roads that have criss-crossed the region. It seems to follow an obvious line directly related to the natural contours of the land, keeping very much to the edge of the escarpment. The same is true of the main prehistoric trackways, which also kept to the ridges, well clear of the heavy clays and dense undergrowth of the valleys.

The Romans paid little heed to natural geography. Their roads were famous for going straight from place to place and the routes can still be followed today. Roman roads were built with care, raised up on a bank or aggar, with drainage ditches on either side, and surfaced with stone and gravel. Ryknild Street, which ran from the Cotswolds into Staffordshire, crosses the walk near Chipping Campden, while the Ermin Way climbs the scarp face near Birdlip. Neither road, however, has made as great an impact on the landscape as have the major routes centred on Cirencester. Perhaps the greatest tribute that can be paid to the Roman builders is the fact that modern engineers have found no better routes for their own roads than those laid down by their predecessors, working nearly 2,000 years ago.

## The Dark Ages

Little is known about life in the region during the so-called Dark Ages that lasted from the end of the Roman occupation to the Norman Conquest. They are 'dark' not because they were periods of unusual anarchy and violence, but due to the shortage of written records to illuminate the period. For a time, life continued much as it had during the Roman occupation. Evidence suggests that Crickley Hill fort, for example, was home to a hamlet that survived until at least the 6th century. Trade continued, especially in such essential commodities as salt, which was vital as a preservative. As early as the 8th century, the King of Mercia had granted the church at Worcester a plot of ground for salt houses in Droitwich. Radiating from the latter were a number of routes, known as the salt ways. One of these routes passed close to Winchcombe, and is still remembered in the names Salter's Lane and Salter's Hill.



## The Middle Ages

In medieval times one theme came to dominate the life of the area: the rearing of sheep for their fleece for the manufacture of woollen cloth. The Cotswold sheep is a distinctive breed, but one that has changed considerably over the centuries. Originally it was an animal noted for its very fine wool, but a breeding programme established in the 18th century with the introduction of

*Nympsfield long barrow: this Neolithic burial site would once have been covered by a large earthen mound, but now the burial chambers are exposed.*

*Selsley church, with its unusual saddleback roof tower, is a prominent landmark on the escarpment above the Stroud valley.*

Leicester rams resulted in the modern breed, a sturdy animal with a dense, heavy fleece. The new breed had better meat than the old, but the main interest in the area was traditionally centred on the wool trade.

The 13th century saw a great expansion in sheep-rearing, the impetus coming from across the Channel in Flanders, where a thriving cloth industry was demanding more and more wool. Indeed, so popular was Cotswold wool that records show merchants coming from as far away as Italy to buy fleeces. Land that had once been ploughed for crops was turned back to grazing for the sturdy Cotswold sheep, leaving the old ridge and furrow as a pattern still visible under the grass. The demand from Flanders declined during the next century, but by now the wool merchants were rich enough and confident enough to begin cloth manufacture on their own account. The area was ideally situated. There was ample grazing and clear water for washing fleeces. The humid climate was ideal for working the wool into yarn and weaving it into cloth. The finished cloth was 'fulled', treated with fuller's earth, plentifully available in the region, to remove the grease, then pounded in water to shrink and felt it, creating a tight weave. Originally, this was done by men walking up and down on the cloth (the origin of the common surname Walker). After fulling, the nap of the cloth was raised using spiky teasel heads, then cut smooth with shears. It could be sold as white cloth, or coloured using local dyes such as woad. In time, the Stroud area became famous for its scarlet cloth. The finished cloth was sent on its way from what was then Britain's second-busiest port, Bristol.

At first, cloth-making was very much a cottage industry, dependent on vast numbers of home spinners and hand-loom weavers. Gradually, however, mechanisation was introduced. This began in medieval times with the fulling mill, in which giant hammers, powered by a waterwheel, did the job of the walkers. For centuries, fulling mills were the only textile mills.

The wealth of the region was intimately associated with the Church. Although there are few imposing monastic remains in the region, this does not mean that there were no grand abbeys nor that the Church was not a powerful institution. The abbeys were among the most powerful landowners and by the end of the 13th-century the Abbey of Gloucester had a flock of 10,000 sheep roaming the Cotswolds. An equally large flock belonged to the more modest Abbey at Winchcombe. Tewkesbury Abbey owned a mill and weaving workshops at Stanway, which walkers will pass on the Way. These and most other monastic houses were destroyed during the reign of Henry VIII. The remains of Hailes Abbey give an idea of its extent and wealth, while a 16th-century gatehouse is the only surviving fragment of Kingswood Abbey, its elaborate carving hinting at the opulence that has been lost. Monastic life was eventually resumed, and the modern Abbey of Prinknash, pronounced for some bizarre reason as 'Prinish', stands in attractive grounds very close to the Way.

The great abbey church that marks one end of the Cotswold Way straddles the decades either side of Henry VIII's Dissolution of the monasteries. Bath Abbey was founded in 1499 and was left unfinished during Henry's reign, its stained-glass windows vandalised, its roof stripped of lead. Work began again under Elizabeth I and was finally completed in the 17th century.

The abbeys owed much of their wealth to their ownership of great flocks and of the land on which they grazed. The churches in turn benefited from the generosity of clothiers and wool merchants, who spent a good deal of their fortunes on church buildings. William Grevel, who died in 1401, is described in his memorial brass as 'the flower of the wool merchants of all England'. He left 100 marks towards the rebuilding of Chipping Campden church. Others were no less generous, and the result is a succession of churches built or extended during the late-medieval period, in the style known as Perpendicular. It is easy to see how the name came about. Everywhere the emphasis is on the vertical: on tall towers, on decorative details such as mouldings that run from floor to roof and, most importantly, on immense high windows. Chipping Campden perfectly demonstrates those qualities.

## Before the Industrial Age

This was a period of increasing prosperity, which saw the construction of some of the great houses that can be seen from the Cotswold Way. The Dissolution of the monasteries by Henry VIII saw an increase in secular power and wealth at the expense of the Church. Stanway Manor had belonged to Tewkesbury Abbey for 800 years, but in the 16th century it was acquired by the Tracy family, who began the present magnificent house. Snowshill Manor was also begun circa 1500. The increasing wealth of the cloth and woollen trade saw a number of fine merchants' houses, examples of which are to be found in almost every town. They endowed almshouses, such as the beautiful 17th-century group in Wotton-under-Edge, embellished old churches and founded new. Churchyards supply ample evidence of the wealth of many of the citizens, and nowhere is this more obvious than in Painswick. In among the clipped yews – traditionally there were always 99 trees – are ornate table tombs, many of them dating from the late 17th century. But in looking at the grand, one should not forget the more humble, vernacular architecture. The classic Cotswold style of cottage and farmhouse was formed during this period.

## The Industrial Age

By far the most important feature for life in the Cotswolds was the mechanisation of the textile industry. It began with the finishing process. The fulling mill had been in use for centuries, but now it was the turn of another aspect of cloth finishing, the raising of the nap. In the gig mill, teasels were mounted on drums, turned by waterwheel, and the cloth ran over them, the spikes pulling up the threads. The next stage was to mechanise the shearing by the use of rotating blades. The latter proved an inspiration to Edwin Budding of Stroud, who in the 19th century adapted the rotating blades and invented the lawnmower. Examples of waterwheel, gig mill and cutter can be seen at work in Dunkirk Mill, between Nailsworth and Stroud, and early lawnmowers are on show in The Museum in the Park in Stroud. The greatest changes came in the 18th century, when the spinning wheel of the cottage was replaced by the machinery of the mill, and, inevitably, the power loom took over from the hand loom. Soon textile mills were spreading out along every available stream. The early mills were often indistinguishable in their outward appearance from the older grain mills, with the same busy waterwheel and simple stone building with stone-slate roof.

The 19th century brought a new source of power, the steam engine, but the waterwheel was far from redundant. One of the grandest of the new generation of mills was Stanley Mill at King's Stanley, which was built in 1813 with five waterwheels and just one steam engine. It was worked in partnership with nearby Ebley Mill, built in the style of a French château. Stanley Mill is still at work, though now producing different materials, but Ebley has been converted into council offices. The decline of the woollen industry began in the late 19th century. High tariffs made it harder to sell cloth abroad and there was increasingly fierce competition from the highly mechanised, modern mills of Yorkshire. One by one the woollen mills closed. Along the southern section of the Cotswold Way there are many fine old mill buildings to be seen, with their mill ponds and sluices. Sadly, the rattle of loom and shuttle has now all but vanished from the Cotswold valleys.

The steam power that served the mills also brought a new transport system to the region – the railway. Brunel's Great Western led the way and his line, linking Cheltenham to Swindon and London, is still very much in use, and is crossed by the path at Stonehouse. Other lines were lost in the latter part of the 20th century, but some at least have come back to life, if not necessarily in their original form. Steam trains roll once again on part of the line between Cheltenham and Stratford-upon-Avon, but the old branch line to Nailsworth now has quieter traffic, serving as footpath and cycle track. New roads have brought increased traffic to the area and have created a brand-new industry: tourism. Some of the more popular towns, such as Broadway, enjoy huge numbers of visitors. But if today it sometimes seems easier to buy a Chippendale chair than a loaf of bread in the more popular spots, nothing has happened fundamentally to change the robust charms of the Cotswolds. Walkers on the Cotswold Way may not have history in mind when they set off, but it is the changes brought by man to countryside and town that have combined to make this a uniquely enjoyable journey.

*Looking across to Downham Hill from Cam Long Down.*

PART TWO

# Cotswold Way

# 1 Chipping Campden to Broadway

*6 miles (9.6 km)*

*Parking: Back Ends, grid reference: SP 152395, no charge*

**Ascent** 567 feet (173 metres)
**Descent** 790 feet (241 metres)
**Lowest point** Broadway 279 feet (85 metres)
**Highest point** Broadway Tower 1,027 feet (313 metres)



Chipping Campden is a fine market town, dominated by a magnificent church **1**, but the Cotswold Way does not begin there. It has its official start at the Market Hall **2**, as recorded on a plaque. Continue down the main street to the Catholic Church **A**. Turn up the side street by the church and, where the road swings round to the right, turn left past a very attractive thatched cottage. At the end of the road continue on up the rough track, past an orchard on the left. Over to the left there is a first glimpse of one of the next objectives, Broadway Tower. Go past the farm buildings and continue uphill on the bridleway. This early part of the walk is like the overture to some major work, introducing all the

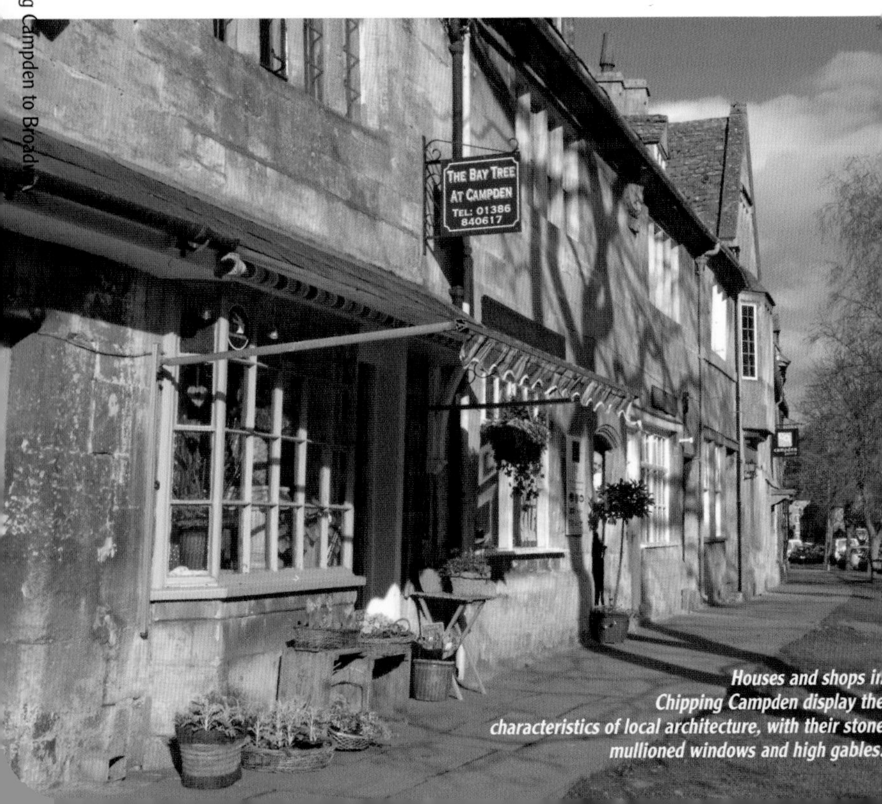


*Houses and shops in Chipping Campden display the characteristics of local architecture, with their stone mullioned windows and high gables.*

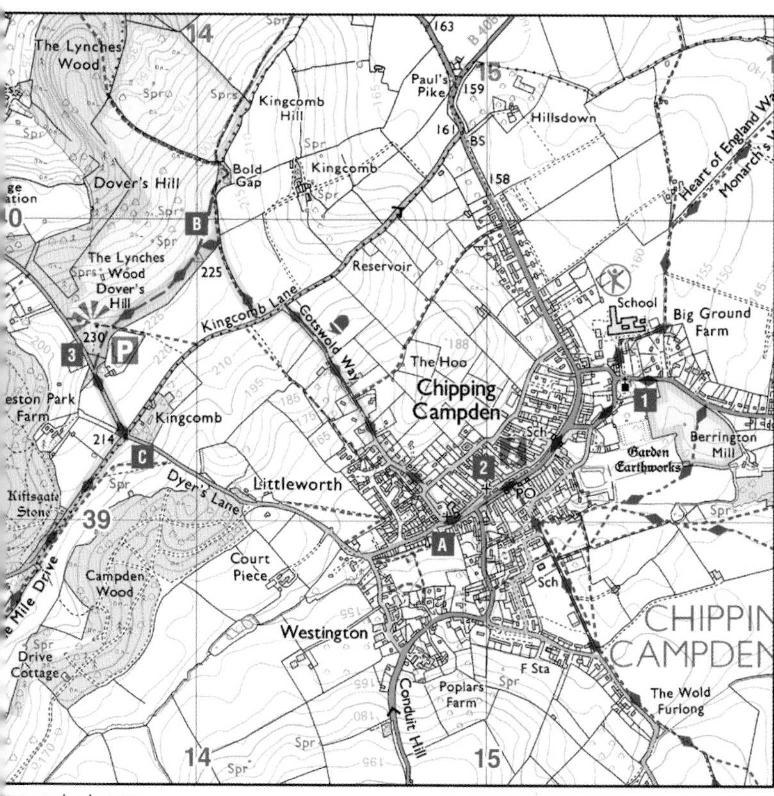

ours are given in metres
vertical interval is 5m

themes that will be developed later. Having left the ideal Cotswold town, one is now introduced to Cotswold farmland, fields speckled with stone. Turn left at the road and, 100 yards on, turn right to continue along the footpath at the side of the hedge, which leads up to the grassland at the top of the escarpment. Here is one of those magnificent panoramas which are such a feature of the Cotswold Way, looking out across the Vale of Evesham. Equally typical is the fact that this is a place with a story to tell. Around 1612 Robert Dover instituted annual games here at Dover's Hill, under the grand title of the Olimpick Games (see page 43).

The walk turns left **B** to follow the line of the hedge over a wide expanse of turf. Along the way is a trig. point and a topograph **3** – again, the first of many – indicating what can be seen in the surrounding landscape. At the end of the grassland, go through the car park to the roadway and turn left. At the crossroads **C**, turn right. A short way down the road on the right is the Kiftsgate Stone, marking a moot or meeting place, where locals gathered to discuss their affairs as far back as Saxon times. Where the road begins to turn right carry straight on down the footpath, which leads to a wide, grassy track. This is the Mile Drive, extending like some great processional way, with hedgerows to either side. Over to the left is a view of Campden

***Heraldic shields of the Earls of Gloucester and Gainsborough at Chipping Campden.***



House and its surrounding parkland. At the end of the Drive, go through the obvious gap in the stone wall and take the path across the field. Cross the road and the next stone stile to continue across the field, heading towards the prominent clump of trees. Once this would all have been grassland, but modern technology has made it possible to cultivate the stony soil. Because this is a comparatively new development, the fields are all very big, not divided into the small units of the older agricultural systems. At the end of the field system **D**, go through the gate and turn left through the picnic area. At the end of the trees, drop down into the car park. Turn right just before the information boards and toilets and climb the grassy bank to the road. Cross the road and continue up the road towards the quarry. Continue past the quarry entrance and then take the path through the wood. This is typical of much of the woodland along the way, dominated by imposing beech trees and carpeted with aromatic ramson, the wild garlic. Leave the wood by the kissing-gate and continue straight on over grassland. Here the view opens out across the Vale of Evesham to Bredon Hill. This open land at the escarpment edge is just the place to look out for birds of prey, such as buzzards, which announce their presence by their distinctive mewing call. The track is quite well defined, and is waymarked by posts. Soon Broadway Tower itself again appears; it is approached along a little dry valley, from which one emerges to be faced by one of the great panoramas of the Cotswold Way.

Broadway Tower **4** is an undeniably handsome building, but more than a little quirky. The battlements are no doubt meant to suggest some great medieval fortress, but the round-headed windows and dainty balconies give it an almost cosy air. The view from the top is scarcely different from that at the bottom, so why was it built? The answer, as with so many follies, would seem to be to impress the neighbours. It was constructed around 1800 to a design by James Wyatt for the Earl of Coventry, but the Countess seems to have been the enthusiast behind the scheme. It was said that before construction began she ordered a beacon to be lit on the top of the hill, and was then driven throughout the surrounding countryside to make sure everyone could see it. The tower is open to visitors, but is only accessed from the walk by means of a detour through the deer park.

The walk continues to the right, round the fence enclosing the tower, before heading off downhill. The escarpment now falls away quite steeply and walking is made easier by a short flight of steps.

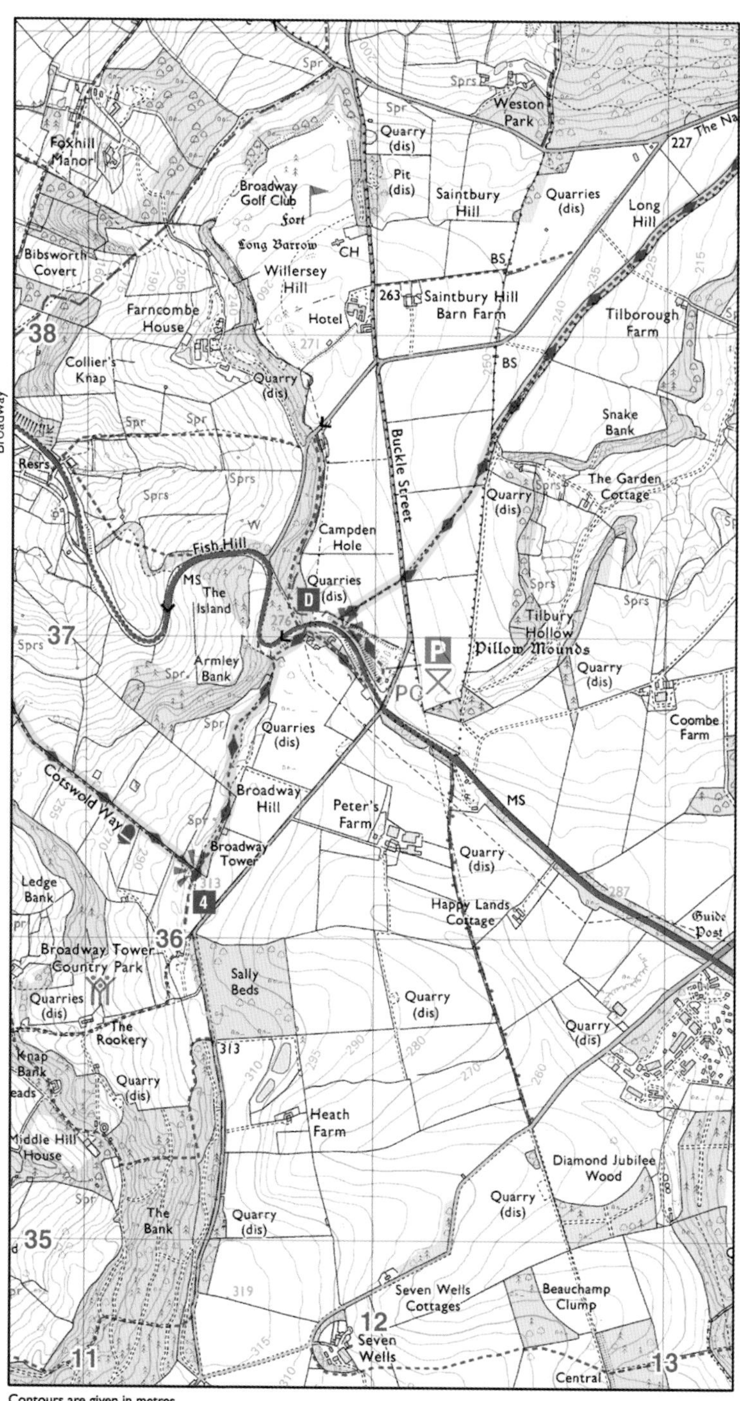


Contours are given in metres
The vertical interval is 5m

*Broadway Tower is a magnificent folly, built around 1800, not for any specific purpose but rather more to impress the neighbours.*

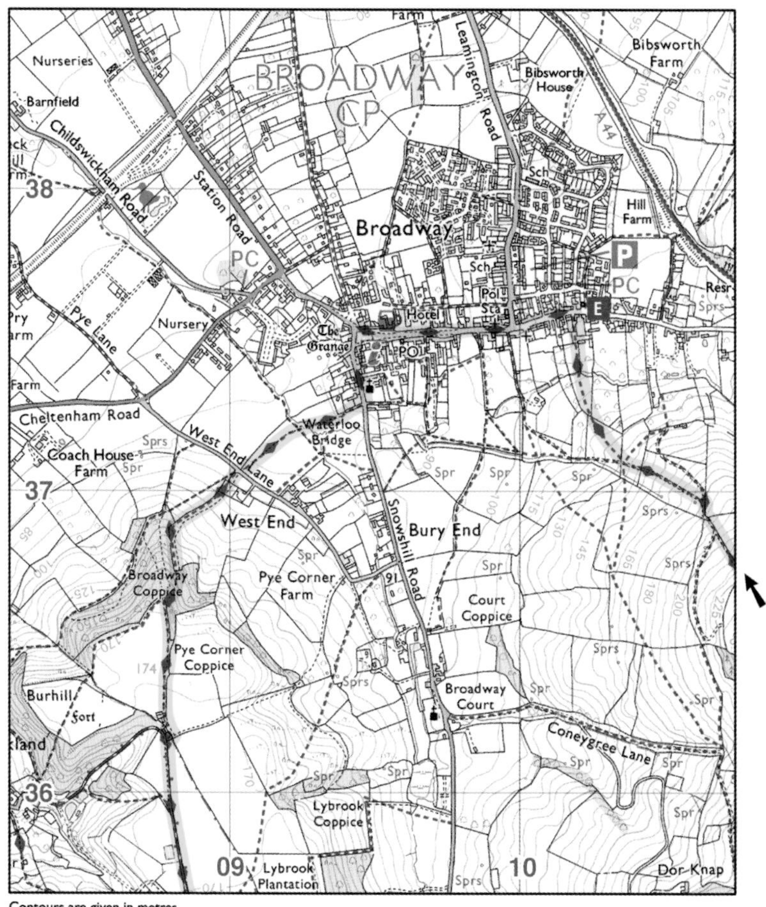


Contours are given in metres
The vertical interval is 5m

The path continues past a recently restored drystone wall – it is always a pleasure to see old crafts still being used, particularly when the work is done as well as it is here. Having crossed the stile by the wooden gate, do not take the broad track that swings round to the right, but continue straight on across the grassland, through a series of gates, as marked by the line of posts. Over to the right is a fine example of ridge and furrow. In medieval times, fields were divided into narrow strips, and as the same strip was ploughed over and over again, so the ridges grew ever higher. When at a later date the field was grassed and turned over to pasture, the old pattern was retained as if in a fossilised landscape. At the bottom of the hill, where paths divide, take the path to the right. Approaching the houses, go through the kissing-gate beside the farm gate **E** and take the narrow lane, leading out to the road where you turn left for the centre of Broadway.

# Chipping Campden

Anyone beginning at the precise starting point of the Cotswold Way will actually miss the best of this magnificent town, where architectural magnificence sits comfortably beside mellow vernacular buildings of great charm. So this brief description is for all those prepared to walk a few extra hundred yards to make a start by the parish church.

The church of St James **1** is one of those glorious Perpendicular churches, paid for out of the profits of a thriving wool trade. It is approached along an avenue of lime trees, six to each side, representing the twelve Apostles. Both inside and out, the eye is constantly drawn upwards – by the strong verticals of the mouldings on the tower, and by the clerestory windows accentuating the shimmering richness of interior decoration, particularly on

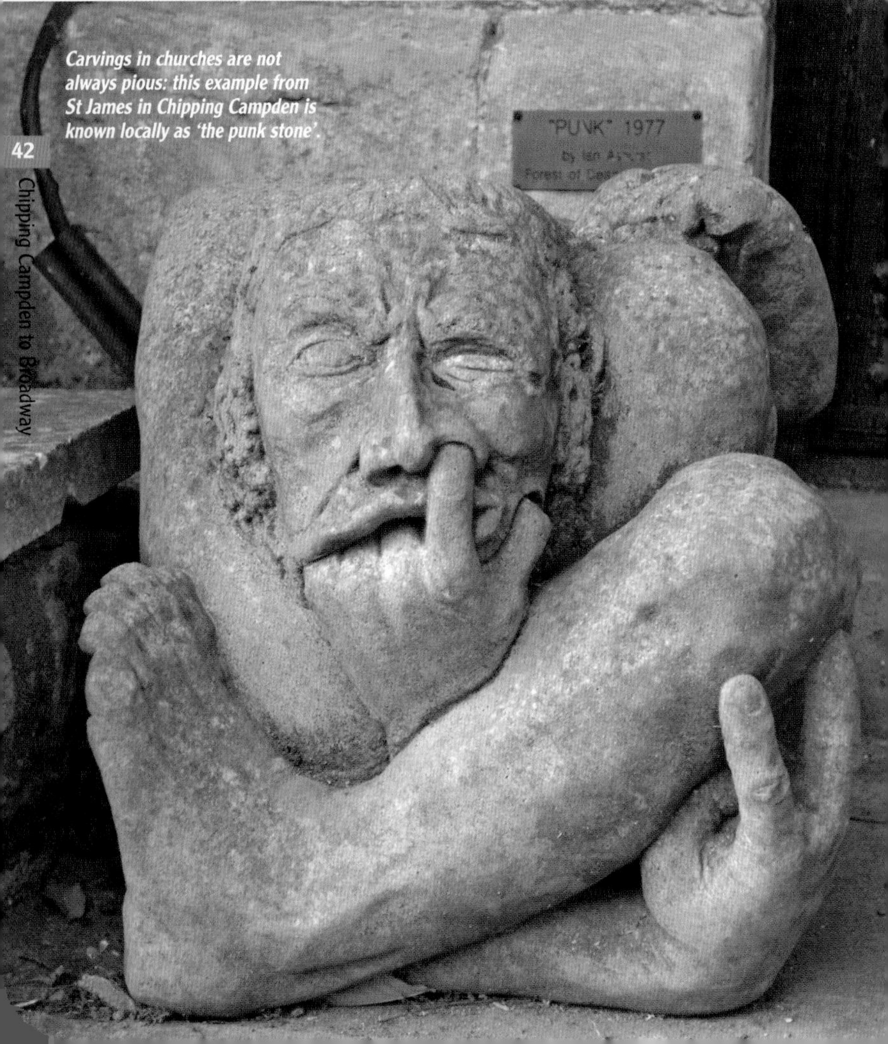


*Carvings in churches are not always pious: this example from St James in Chipping Campden is known locally as 'the punk stone'.*

the tombs. The alabaster effigies of Sir Baptist and Lady Elizabeth Hicks present a picture of grandeur, frozen and immortalised.

Leaving the church, one finds a wealth of fine architecture on view. Over to the left is the very ornate entrance to what was once Sir Baptist Hicks's old Campden House. Built in 1613, it was destroyed by retreating Royalists in the Civil War: 'the house which was so faire, burnt', as one account records. All that remains are the East and West Banqueting Houses, a riot of pinnacles and gables. Opposite are the modest, but no less attractive, almshouses. The miracle of Chipping Campden is that so many styles can live so comfortably together, unified by the local stone and a long tradition. Bedford House with its pilasters, cornices and cheeky cherubs does not look out of place, even when set against 14th-century buildings such as Grevel House and Woolstaplers' Hall. In the main street is a last reminder of Sir Baptist Hicks: the Market Hall **2** he endowed. The building offers an opportunity to see just how a stone roof is constructed, for the underside is all exposed.

## The Olimpick Games

Dover's Olimpick Games became famous, so much so that a book about them was published in 1636, including descriptions of the activities and poems by such luminaries as Ben Jonson. A castle was constructed on the hill and guns were fired to start the proceedings. There were some familiar events – running, jumping and dancing – but others certainly have no place in the modern Olympics. Backswords, coursing and pike-tumbling have long been forgotten, but others are at least recognisable, such as sack races – except unlike sack races at modern fêtes, the competitors here had the sacks tied up to their necks.

The games lasted through to 1852, when they were ended because they didn't match Victorian notions of respectability. But they were restarted in 1951 as part of the Festival of Britain celebrations, and the spirit of the old games lingers on. The castle is still built every year, and the event ends with a torchlight procession into the town. Even some of the older games have survived, including the alarming-sounding shin-kicking contests. The Olimpicks begin on the Friday after the Spring Bank Holiday. The games may not have the prestige of the international competition, but they are probably a lot more fun.

## The Arts and Crafts movement

The Arts and Crafts movement was begun in the 19th century as a reaction to the filth, squalor and degradation that seemed to be inseparable from the relentless advance of industrialisation. In fine art it was closely allied to the Pre-Raphaelite call for a return to nature as the only true inspiration for art. For the craftsman it represented a turning away from over-elaborate design and from the world of machines. One of the great leaders of the movement was William Morris, poet, architect, textile and book designer, and

*This stained-glass window in Selsley church was the work of the most famous of the Arts and Crafts studios, set up by William Morris.*

much else. He expressed his personal philosophy as follows:

'Never forget the material you are working with, and try always to use it for what it can do best; if you feel yourself hampered by the material in which you are working, instead of being helped by it, you have so far not learned your business, any more than a would-be poet has, who complains of the hardship of writing in measure and rhyme.'

Not surprisingly, Morris fell in love with the Cotswolds, an area where tradition survived and where buildings perfectly demonstrate respect for local materials. With his friends Dante Gabriel Rossetti and Edward Burne-Jones, he often stayed in Broadway Tower, and in 1871 he took a lease on Kelmscott Manor, a name which became famous through the beautifully produced books of the Kelmscott Press.

Morris was more than just a theorist. 'The Firm' he established produced a range of products from wallpapers to stained-glass windows (examples of these can be seen in Selsley church, near Stroud). His enthusiastic disciples included Ernest Gimson, who set up his workshops at Daneway House, Sapperton, in 1902, making hand-crafted furniture. Gimson's modestly stated aim was to produce work that was 'useful and right, pleasantly shaped and finished, good enough, but not too good for ordinary use'. In fact, his craftsmen created furniture which stands proudly in a great English tradition. Other craftsmen, too, made their way to the Cotswolds. In 1902 C. R. Ashbee arrived in Chipping Campden with an entire London guild of handicraft workers, 150 people in all, and moved into premises in Sheep Street. Another important furniture factory was set up by Gordon Russell in Broadway, with headquarters in a 16th-century building, now a guest house and restaurant, Russell's of Broadway.

William Morris's concern for craftsmanship, materials and tradition extended beyond making beautiful things for his contemporaries. He was an equally passionate defender of the beauties of the past. The Victorian age saw a great rush towards the 'restoration' of ancient churches, but all too often this led to the destruction of original features, which were hidden behind the elaborate curlicues and twiddles of the new Gothic. The result, wrote Morris, was to make an old church look like 'a nineteenth-century medieval furniture-dealer's warehouse'. He believed restoration should be limited to keeping out the wet and ensuring the walls remained upright. To promote his ideas he founded the Society for the Protection of Ancient Buildings. It is thanks to Morris and his successors that many of the Cotswold churches have been spared from the heavy hand of the restorer.

***The traditional Cotswold manor house at Kelmscott, once home to William Morris.***

# 2 Broadway to Wood Stanway

*6.5 miles (10.5 km)*

*Parking: Leamington Road, grid reference SP 100377, long stay and toilets, charge*

**Ascent** 813 feet (248 metres)

**Descent** 715 feet (218 metres)

**Lowest point** Broadway 279 feet (85 metres)

**Highest point** Shenberrow Hill 968 feet (295 metres)



Turn left to join the wide main street of Broadway, which is one of the showpieces of the Cotswolds. It is a tourist honey-pot, but one has to remember that tourists come because it really does have a wealth of fine buildings. The overall effect is very impressive, but often it is the individual building – or even the small detail – that catches the eye. No. 68, for example, has an unusual little porch supported on classical, fluted pillars. Houses vary from those in the local style to others with gentrified, bland ashlar frontages. At the end of the main street **A**, turn left on to the Snowshill road. There is still the same rich variety of buildings – including a rarity for this part of the world, a timber-framed cottage with thatched

***Broadway draws many visitors attracted by the rich variety of buildings that line its wide main street.***

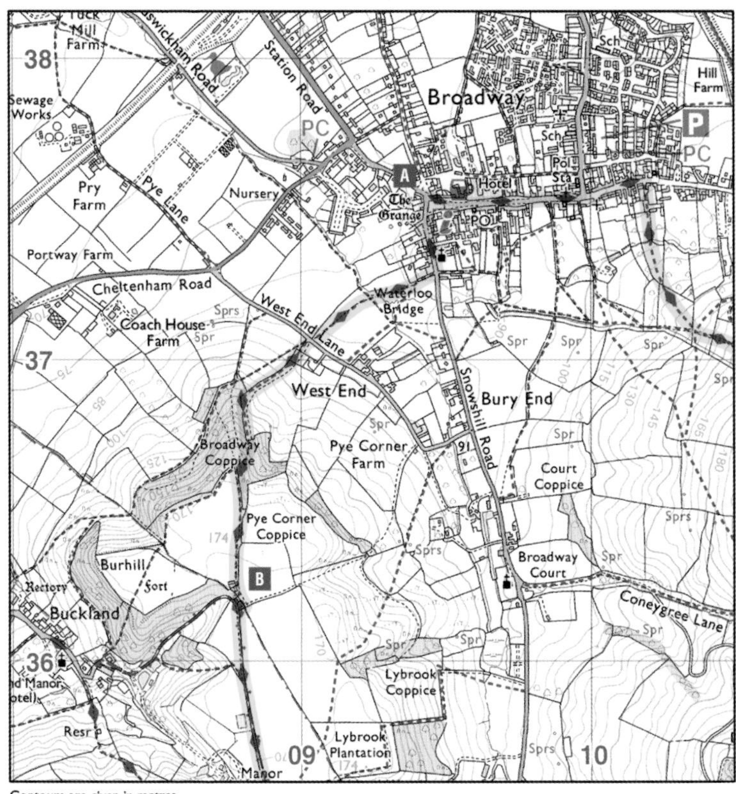

Contours are given in metres
The vertical interval is 5m

roof – and the locals seem to vie with each other for the grandeur of their topiary.

Immediately beyond the church, turn right, crossing the road to take the rough track beside the houses. At the end of the track, go through the gate and head off towards a small footbridge and continue on to the road. Cross straight over and take the path that heads steadily uphill beside the hedge, which seems a popular nesting place for a variety of birds, including chaffinch, greenfinch, robin and wren. Soon the views open up and there is a fine, open prospect, looking back towards Broadway and Broadway Tower. Follow the path up to the top of the hill, then follow the edge of the woodland round to the left. Enter the woods by the gate and continue on along the obvious track winding through the trees, a mixture of oak, ash, birch and coppiced hazel. At the top of the little hill, turn left on to the broader track and leave the wood by the kissing-gate, emerging on to arable land. Follow the track between the edge of the wood and the field and carry straight on. Continue on through the gate, passing the farm buildings to your right. Immediately beyond the barn, turn right through the gate, then turn left on to the broad farm track **B**.

This plateau of farmland seems alternately to echo in summer with the song of skylarks and meadow pipits. Where the ways divide at the top of the little hill, turn right towards Stanton **C**. Those who want to visit nearby Snowshill Manor **5** should turn left at this point.

The route continues on the broad track beside the fence, circling the hill. The way passes a number of fine beech trees and as it steadily climbs, so the limestone bedrock appears as a polished, natural pavement underfoot. This is pleasant, easy walking with wide views out over the Vale of Evesham. The path swings round to the left, past the remains of an old quarry, and there is a brief glimpse of the village of Snowshill, down in the valley.

Here a number of tracks meet **D**, including the return path from Snowshill. Turn right and the path leads through attractively undulating grassland and past a wood that echoes to the raucous calls of pheasants to reach the rather insubstantial embankments that mark the edge of Shenberrow Camp, an Iron Age settlement. At Shenberrow Buildings, go through the gate to the right of the house and follow the track downhill along the hollow, its sides brightened by hawthorn and gorse. Cross a stile and



## Snowshill

Leaving the main walk at the edge of Buckland Wood, carry straight on down the hill keeping the wood on the left. Continue straight on, joining the road by the next area of woodland. Just before the woodland on the right comes to an end, look out for a kissing-gate **A** on the left. Go through the gate and take the path heading downhill beside the fence. On reaching the woodland, take the path that meanders through the trees to cross the stream on a culvert by the ruined bridge. Carry on up the opposite side of the valley, following the fence on the right until you reach a wide, spreading oak **B**. Take the path that leads diagonally up the face of the hill to end at a stile by the road. Turn right on the road into the village of Snowshill.

The road leads past the car park, which is also the entrance to Snowshill Manor **5**, now in the care of the National Trust. This is an almost perfect example of a Cotswold manor house, begun as a long, gabled, narrow house around 1500, and extended in the 17th and 18th centuries. The new work has, however, all been constructed in the same honey-coloured stone, so that only the most expert eye can discern the changes. The inside is equally remarkable, if only for the collection put together by one of the owners, Charles Paget Wade. He was a magpie of a collector, so that one moves from clocks to musical instruments, from bicycles to toys and ends up, for no obvious reason, with Samurai armour.

Beyond the Manor, the cottages that line the street and the old Snowshill Arms inn are typically Cotswold. Continue out of the village on the tree-shaded road. At the road junction turn right up the road, running between banks and hedges, signposted as a dead end. At the next road junction turn right **C**, and there is a fine view out over the village and its valley. After a short way, the road dips. Go through the gate on the left **D** and head diagonally uphill towards the middle of the wood. Go over the stile to enter the wood and continue on the obvious path swinging round to the left. Cross a second stile and continue up the road running up the side of the wood to rejoin the Cotswold Way.

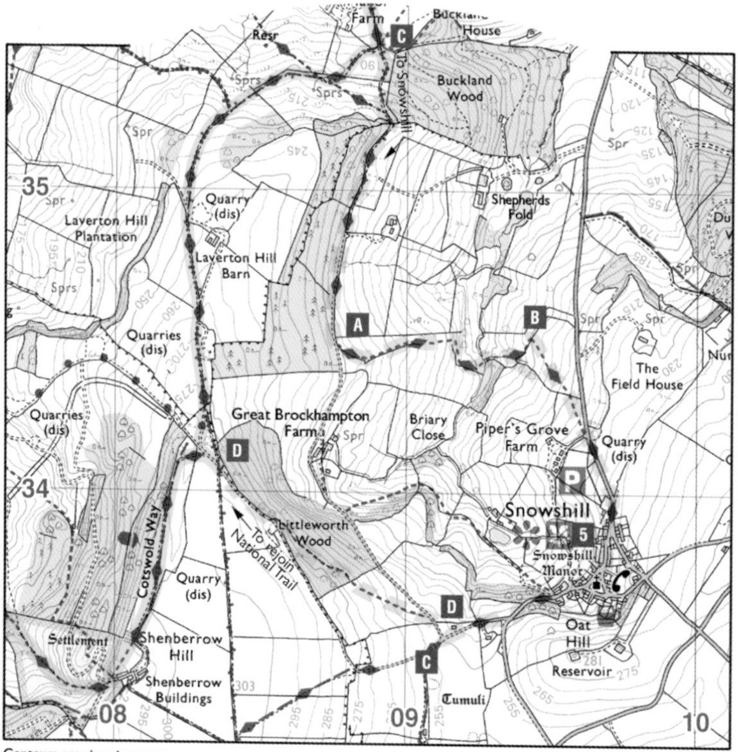

Contours are given in metres
The vertical interval is 5m

A small part of Charles Paget Wade's idiosyncratic collection at Snowshill Manor.

The view down to Stanton from Shenberrow Hill.



continue down the right-hand side of the field, keeping close to the hedge. Cross a small stream and then take the stile to continue downhill. The path turns briefly right to pass above a small pond, then goes through a gate to continue downhill by the stream. Coming out into the open, take the wide track that goes all the way down to the village of Stanton **6**. Turn left towards Stanton, past a lovely pair of cottages, built in stone with high, thatched roofs through which little dormer windows peer. The lane emerges at the green in the centre of Stanton. Thirsty – or hungry – walkers can turn right to visit The Mount Inn, but the Cotswold Way sternly resists temptation, going down the village street to the left.

Stanton is one of those places one hesitates to write about or even mention too loudly, for it has a fragile charm that could all too easily be broken. Here, if anywhere, one feels at the very heart of the Cotswolds, for Stanton has a wealth of superb buildings and not a whiff of pretension. At first sight the church is something of a jumble, both of styles and levels, with odd features such as the dormer window in the roof, peering out among the gargoyles. Inside, there is a surprising serenity and unity, with more grotesque carvings on pillars, an organ loft and rood screen. Beyond the market cross and the church are the imposing gates that lead to Stanton Court. Beyond that is the Manor House, with its traditional mullioned windows and immense external chimney displaying its antiquity, confirmed by the date, 1577, carved over the doorway. Turn left at the road.

Where the road turns round to the right, bear left along the tarmac track on to the bridleway, then turn right through a gate into the field and continue on along the obvious track. A pattern of old ridges and furrows can be seen in the field. Cross over to the next field, then turn slightly right to the gate and continue with the hedge to your left. To the right is a long viaduct, which now carries the Gloucestershire and Warwickshire Railway, once part of the Great Western empire, built in an attempt to ward off territorial attacks by a rival company, the Midland. The occasional blast of a steam whistle echoing across the fields indicates that the line is not all disused – a section has been re-opened as a preserved line running to Cheltenham racecourse, with ambitious plans for future expansion. This is now a very pleasant walk over grassland, with the Way marked by wooden posts. Farmland gradually merges into formal parkland



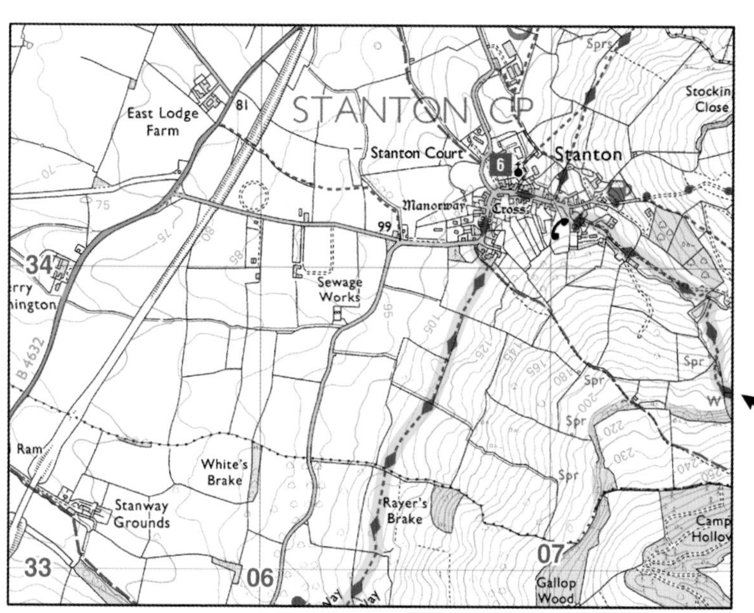


Contours are given in metres
The vertical interval is 5m

with its carefully arranged, yet apparently artless, pattern of fields, hedges and trees, including some magnificent horse chestnut and copper beech. The track heads slightly right to join the road near a little thatched building, which turns out to be the cricket pavilion. It was given to the village by the author J. M. Barrie, who regarded Stanway and cricket with equal enthusiasm.

Turn left on the road which runs past Stanway House **7**, a glorious example of Jacobean architecture. There is also a reminder of former links with Tewkesbury Abbey in the solid form of the great buttressed tithe barn. Among the other outbuildings is the brewhouse, which has recently been brought back into use. It is unusual in having its coppers built over log fires, and the excellent ale is available in a few local

*The path from Stanton to Stanway leads through formal parkland, dotted with some magnificent mature trees.*

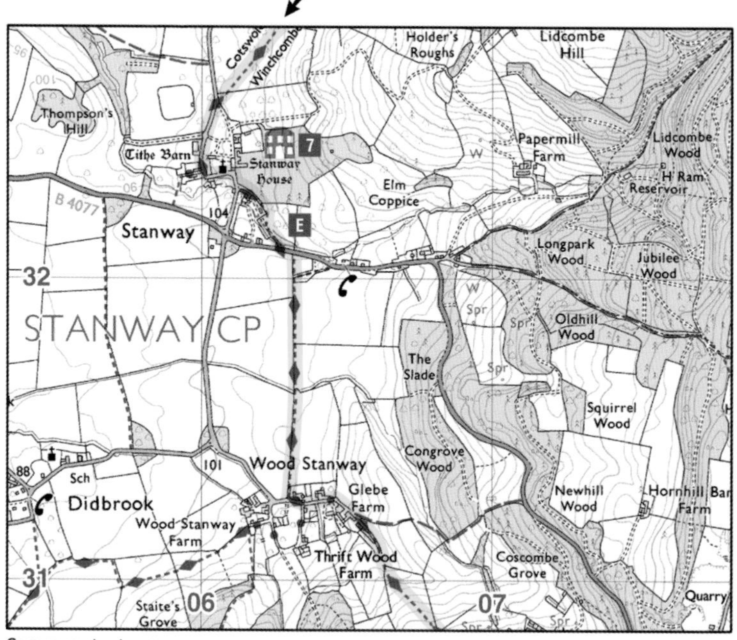


Contours are given in metres
The vertical interval is 5m

pubs. Follow the road as it swings round towards the formal entrance to the house. The extraordinary 17th-century gatehouse features a whole array of architectural devices, including columns, pilasters, pediments and niches. Next to it the church is more modest but still has lovely detail: just look, for example, at the carved heads, which include one very smug-looking gentleman with an upturned moustache. There is a particularly good view of the house (occasionally open to the public) from the churchyard. Another feature of the village is the war monument with crisp lettering by the brilliant typographer and carver Eric Gill.

Beyond the gateway, turn left, passing the building with long windows on the upper floor. Windows like these are an indication that this building was once used by handloom weavers, who needed good light for their work. This was originally the Tewkesbury Abbey mill, and was used for grinding grain as well as fulling cloth. On the ground floor is an internal waterwheel. Unusually, it is overshot – the water arrives by a duct, known as a launder, which can be seen behind the building, and it falls into buckets on the rim of the wheel. This is a very efficient form of waterwheel, and at the time of writing it was undergoing restoration, with the aim of eventually producing flour once again. Next to the old mill is a working blacksmith's forge.

At the end of the footpath, turn left along the road for about 50 yards, then right **E** to take the path running between hedgerows. A stream is crossed on a simple bridge consisting of a single slab of limestone. Turn left on to the road into Wood Stanway.

## Stanway House

The manor originally belonged to the abbey of Tewkesbury, and was purchased by the Tracy family in the 16th century. Much of what we see today dates from the 17th century, but the grounds show the unmistakable imprint of the 18th century. The parkland is very typical of the pastoral idylls made famous by Capability Brown. The magnificent water gardens were probably designed by Charles Bridgeman in the same period, and are being restored. There are four ponds, a formal canal designed as a landscape feature, not for use, and a cascade. Most imposing of all the features is the

*The restored 18th-century water gardens at Stanway House have a new addition – Britain's tallest fountain, throwing its plume a hundred metres into the air.*



gravity fountain, which was completed in 2004. Basically, water is fed from a 100,000 gallon (450,000 litre) reservoir 155 feet (47 metres) above the canal through a 1.5-mile (2-km) pipe, so that when it emerges at the bottom of the hill through a 2-inch (5-cm) nozzle it is under such pressure that it shoots a jet high into the air.

Until recently Witley Court in Worcestershire could claim to have the highest jet fountain in Britain at 121 feet (37 metres), but Stanway has now easily taken the crown. The jet shoots an astonishing 300 feet (91 metres) into the air. Even when walking past the grounds, rather than visiting, this is a sight walkers will certainly not miss.

# 3 Wood Stanway to Winchcombe

*5.4 miles (8.8 km)*

*Parking: no recommended site – please do not attempt to park here. The nearest available site is Stanton Village Hall, grid reference SP067344, charge*

**Ascent** 564 feet (172 metres)
**Descent** 679 feet (207 metres)
**Lowest point** Winchcombe 262 feet (80 metres)
**Highest point** Beckbury Camp 892 feet (272 metres)

Follow the road through the village as it bends to the right, past a farm and pony-trekking centre **A**. Continue straight on past the barns and follow the rough track as it begins to climb uphill, back to the top of the escarpment, waymarked by wooden posts. Look out for a gate in the fence on the left, go through it and continue uphill via the marker posts. Looking back, you can see that this was once ploughed, with marks of ridge and furrow and cultivation terraces on the hillside, known as strip lynchets. Beyond the next gate turn diagonally left towards the farm buildings, then continue following the line of waymarks. At the top of the hill is a bench, which provides a chance to recover from the climb and enjoy a magnificent view out across the Vale.

Turn left along the path beside the stone wall and the line of beech trees, which are home to a clamorous rookery. By the roadway is the stump of a cross, hence the name Stumps Cross **8**. Turn sharp right on to the bridleway that runs by an avenue of trees. Note that the corrugated barn stands on older staddle stones, which keep the structure clear of damp and vermin. The dried-up dew pond has a cross of stone walls, making it accessible from four different fields. At the end of the avenue where ways divide **B** turn right,

***The path along the escarpment near Stumps Cross.***

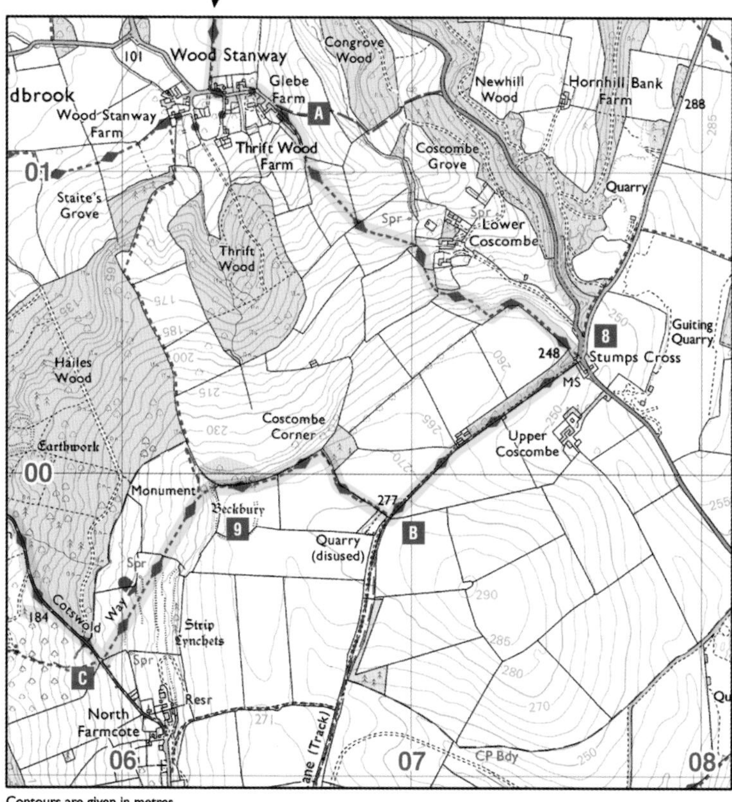

Contours are given in metres
The vertical interval is 5m

go through the gate and keep to the edge of the field with the wall to your right. Continue following the line of the wall as it swings round to the left; it is worth noting how much a well-maintained stone wall like this adds to the character of the scenery. The earthworks on the left are the rampart and partially filled-in ditch of Beckbury Camp **9**, an Iron Age promontory fort. The steep escarpment provides the main defence, and the earthworks close off the neck of the promontory. Passing the end of the fortifications, the path emerges on the edge of the scarp by a stone monument, with a little niche where passers-by can rest. Legend has it that Thomas Cromwell sat here to watch the destruction of Hailes Abbey, but if he did it was not on this monument, which was built much later.

From here the path heads steeply downhill through the trees. The route curves to the left towards a marker post and then heads slightly left towards a gap in the trees. This continues as a pleasant walk across grassland, heading towards a gate by the patch of woodland on the right. Turn diagonally left towards the marker post and continue on to reach the bridleway **C**. Turn right on to the stony path, running past orchards to one side and to the other woodland, which in spring is notable for its masses of bluebells. The

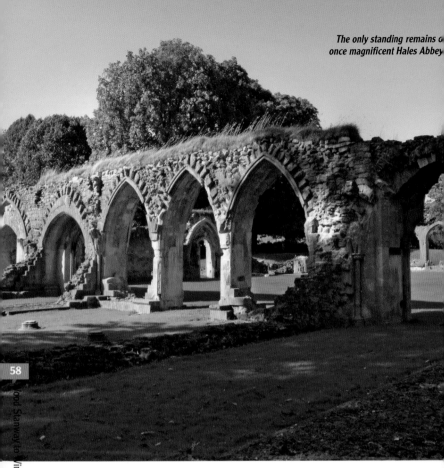

*The only standing remains o*
*once magnificent Hales Abbey*





track goes steeply downhill to emerge by the entrance to the fruit farm. Continue on the road down to Hailes Abbey **10**. This is open to the public, although there is a very good view of the site from the walk. One reason to visit the Abbey is the small but excellent museum which, apart from telling the history of the buildings, has a fascinating exhibition showing the variety of the local stones, ranging from steely blue lias to the familiar golden oolitic limestone. The Abbey was founded in the middle of the 13th century, and was one of the last Cistercian houses in England. Now all that remains are a row of cloister arches,

Contours are given in m
The vertical interval is

part of the chapter house and the foundations telling of a once-great array of buildings. The little church opposite could easily be overlooked, but inside is a splendid set of medieval wall paintings and stained glass rescued from the Abbey.

Turn left opposite Hailes church, through the kissing-gate, and head on a diagonal to the right towards the gate in the corner to the right of the house. Isolated stone fragments and humps in the ground indicate outlying Abbey remains. Turn right on to the road and after about 50 yards, where the road turns round to the right **D**, turn left on to the bridleway, part of the old Pilgrims' Way, linking the Abbey to Winchcombe. Where a footpath turns off, continue straight on along the bridleway. Where tracks meet, turn right on to the green track beside the field and then left on to a well-defined track going straight through the middle of a field of crops. At the far side of the field, cross the stile and turn left, then almost immediately go through a kissing-gate. The path turns on a diagonal away from the fence on the right, through very open country and continues in much the same direction, through a kissing-gate and over a small footbridge. Winchcombe comes into view and you head for a stile in the far downhill corner of the field. Join the lane, then turn left on to the road into Winchcombe.

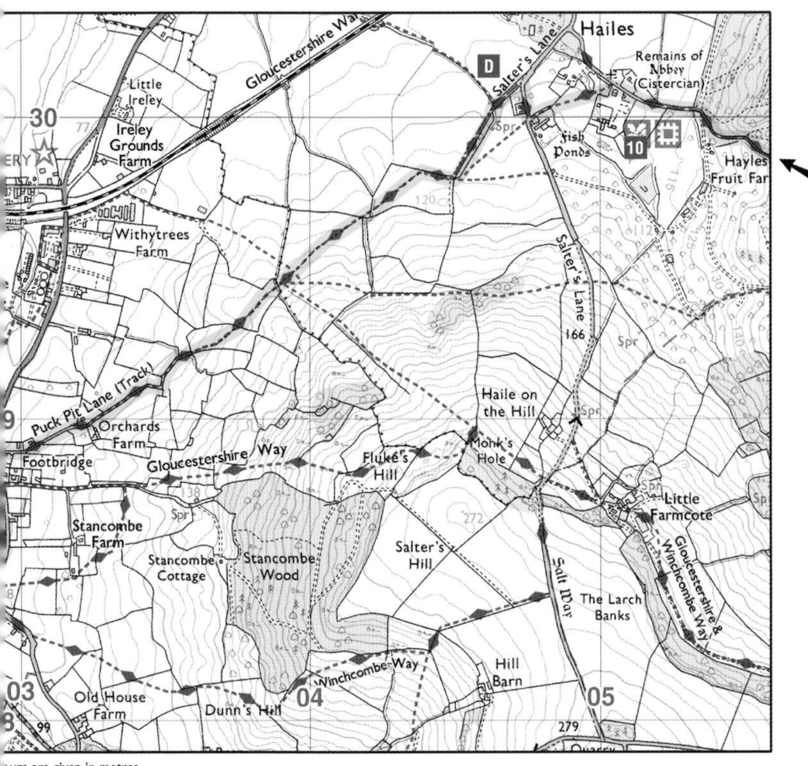


ours are given in metres
vertical interval is 5m

# 4 Winchcombe to Cleeve Hill

*5.6 miles (9.0 km)*
*Parking: Back Lane, grid reference SP 023284, long stay and toilets, no charge*

**Ascent** 1,082 feet (330 metres)
**Descent** 476 feet (145 metres)
**Lowest point** Winchcombe 262 feet (80 metres)
**Highest point** Belas Knapp 968 feet (295 metres)

Winchcombe has buildings not just of great character, but of great variety. Timber-framed houses stand next to others of substantial stone. Almost immediately you pass a typical high-gabled Cotswold house, closely followed by a jettied, timber-framed building that looks as if it has strayed across from another county. Dent's Terrace almshouses fit in snugly, but are rather exotic, with different coloured stones creating patterned arches – a clue to their Victorian origin, designed by one of the most famous architects of the age, Sir Giles Gilbert Scott. Queen's Square has the best of the secular architecture in the Jacobean House (1619). Inevitably, the grandest building is the church **11**, just slightly off the walk – another example of the Perpendicular style. Outside is a fearsome array of gargoyles; strange beasts snarl down, while monsters with hideous faces glower out over the churchyard. These mythological horrors were once matched in real life: bullet marks show where Royalist prisoners were lined up and shot in the Civil War. The interior of the church contains a particularly fine polychrome monument, in a delightful naïve style, to Thomas Williams, buried in 1636. The town also has an interesting local museum and a wonderfully bizarre railway museum, where signals wag above the cabbages.

Beyond Queens Square **A**, turn left down Vineyard Street (once known as Duck Street, as there was a ducking stool by the river at the bottom). Across the bridge is a barn, packed with ecclesiastical details, which might well have come from the old Abbey after the Dissolution. At the end of the road is the gateway to Sudeley Castle **12**. Dating from the 14th century, it eventually succumbed to the fate of so many English castles in the aftermath of the Civil War. Left in ruins in 1649, it was bought in 1810 and a few years later the long work of restoration began. It is now a handsome set of buildings which are open to the public.

Once across the bridge, turn right through the gate into the field, then turn diagonally to the left, following paths down the edges of the field. From here there is a clear pathway across the field, and a good view across to the castle. Cross a bridge over a stream and follow the path to the right round the edge of the field. Beyond the next gate, continue along the hedge. At the roadway turn left, then right down the imposing driveway to Corndean Hall. Once past the manicured cricket pitch, where the driveway swings right **B**, turn left by the fingerpost and take the path on the right heading diagonally up the hill. A marker post soon comes into view, the first of a whole series pointing the way up this steep climb. The exercise is rewarded by a fine view. Go through the gate, and cross straight over the road, and turn left to go through a second gate **C** that leads to a path at the edge of the woodland.

Follow the path as it swings round to the right to go uphill through the strip of woodland, then turn left and continue to follow the edge of the field. Go through the gate and follow the boundary wall beside the patch of dense woodland. The high mound of Belas Knap **13** appears up ahead. The name means 'beacon mound' but this

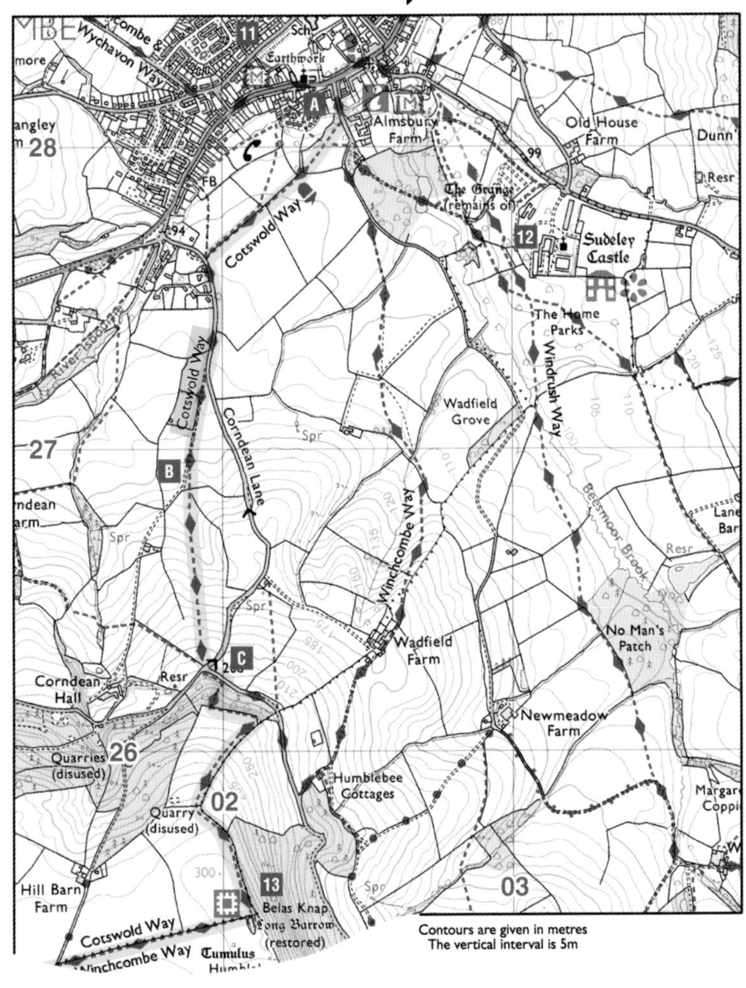

is, in fact, a Neolithic chambered long barrow. It has what appears to be a very impressive entrance: a forecourt which curves out to a horn shape is surrounded by drystone walls, at the centre of which are two uprights and a lintel. But it is all false: nothing lies behind the 'door' except a large blocking stone. The actual entrances are at the side and lead to four small burial chambers, which were found to contain an estimate of at least 30 skeletons. The false entrance may be stylistic or might simply mark the end of its period of use, but as the people who lived here some 4,000 years ago left no written records, we have no means of knowing.

Leave the enclosure by the stile, returning now to the landscape of the plateau, with extensive fields neatly divided by stone walls. At the end of a rather dull trudge beside fields, join the broad track that runs between thicket hedges. A route change is planned for this section, so please keep an eye out for the signs. In this somewhat featureless section of the walk, birds often provide the main interest. Thrushes nest in the hedges, and one might hear the tuneful song of the wheatear, a summer visitor from Africa. Shortly before reaching the farm buildings, turn right by the Cotswold Way signpost **D** to follow the path beside the field that leads straight down to the woodland. Enter the wood and take the obvious path, which soon swings round to the right. This is the oddly named Breakheart Plantation, and no one appears certain just whose heart was broken. It is based on ancient woodland, but it now offers a delightful easy stroll on a clearly defined path through a mixture of young and mature, mostly broad-leaved, trees. The path passes an old limestone quarry, before reaching the edge of the wood at the end of a minor road. Turn sharp left to cross the narrow neck of woodland and leave the wood.

The path now continues across the fields on a bridleway heading towards another patch of woodland and the tiny hamlet of Postlip. The track soon arrives at the first of the buildings, the typical Cotswold farmhouse of Postlip Hall Farm. Where the track is in use, for example for moving farm animals, you are allowed to take the short path through the field to the left of the farmyard. Continue along the farm road then turn left, with the boundary wall of Postlip Hall on your right. This is a historic grouping, centred on the Hall itself, which is a fine example of a multi-gabled Cotswold manor house, dating back to

### The Cotswold Lion

**This was the name given to the old breed of Cotswold sheep, notable for its fine, long fleece and rather shaggy appearance. Its wool was greatly prized, but was later replaced by imported Merino wool. Sheep still graze Cleeve Common, but the Cotswold is now a rare breed.**

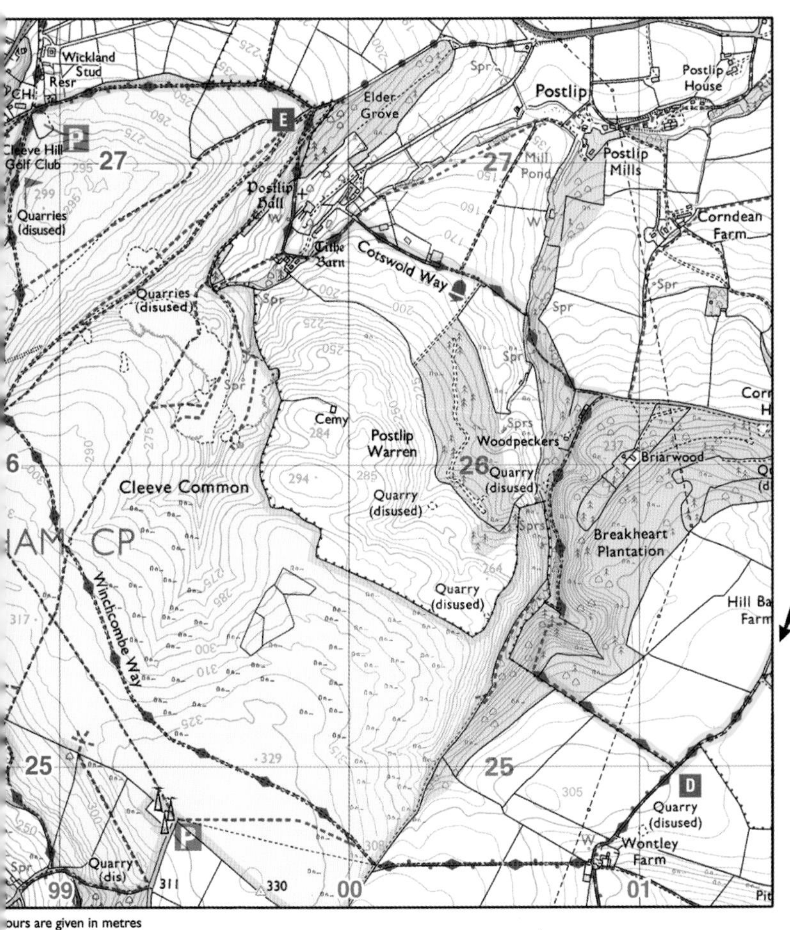


ours are given in metres
vertical interval is 5m

the 14th century, though most of the present building is from the late 16th and early 17th centuries. The private chapel is mainly 12th century, with the addition of a later bell turret and the stone tithe barn is probably 15th century. Keep following the wall round to the right then head at an angle up the hill towards the tip of a patch of woodland. There are a number of gates to go before you reach the first patch of open ground at the edge of Cleeve Common. Take the left fork **E** onto the short by-way. At the end of the by-way, go through the gate to turn back onto the common. This is an attractive area for walking, with grass cropped short by the wandering sheep. The path heads uphill along the edge of the common towards the golf clubhouse. As you climb, the view opens out and there are views back to Postlip Hall and a panorama that also takes in Winchcombe and Sudeley Castle. The track arrives at the top of the hill at a quarry and car park.

*Cleeve Hill rising up above the Vale of Gloucester.*

# 5 Cleeve Hill to Dowdeswell

*5.5 miles (8.9 km)*

*Parking: Quarry near golf club, Grid Reference SO 989271, no charge*

**Ascent** 285 feet (87 metres)

**Descent** 564 feet (237 metres)

**Lowest point** Dowdeswell Reservoir 377 feet (115 metres)

**Highest point** 1,000 feet (305 metres)

From the quarry above the golf clubhouse **A** continue following the obvious double track. Cleeve Common represents one of the great unimproved areas of grassland in the Cotswolds, crossed by a complex pattern of unfenced tracks and footpaths. In spite of the incongruous appearance of golf greens scattered around between the patches of rougher grass, this remains a good place to see and hear birds. The meadow pipit is common, easily recognised by its rather feeble song as it rises, which gives way to a more tuneful melody as it parachutes back to earth on outspread wings. By contrast, a less melodic mewing call is the cue to look upwards to find a soaring buzzard. Rabbits are to be seen scampering everywhere. The wildlife together with the wide vistas make this is a very rewarding section to walk. Because of the web of paths, however, walkers have to keep a sharp eye out for marker posts to keep to the Way.

Where tracks divide, keep to the right on the broad, sandy path, passing through an area which has been extensively quarried over the years. Look out for the next marker post **B**, where the route turns left off the obvious track to follow a far less distinct green path up the grassy hill, studded with gorse. The route is clearly marked by posts, and after running diagonally up the hill for most of the way, finally swings round to head directly for the summit. The top is marked by a trig. point and a panorama table **14** identifying all the sites to be seen from one of the finest viewpoints on the Cotswold Way. The most prominent site is Cheltenham, with its racecourse and a somewhat incongruous tower block, built for a local insurance company, plonked in the middle of this mainly Regency town.

Turn right at the panorama and take the path to the right of the golf green, cross a little dip and head for a post by a bench on the skyline. The track now stays close to the edge of the escarpment, which falls away sharply to a line of craggy rock. It arrives at the earthworks of a promontory fort **15**, constructed in the Iron Age, and a rather grander version of Beckbury Camp. This fort was protected by two semicircular ramparts with external ditches. Beyond the fort, the route swings round to the left. Where the

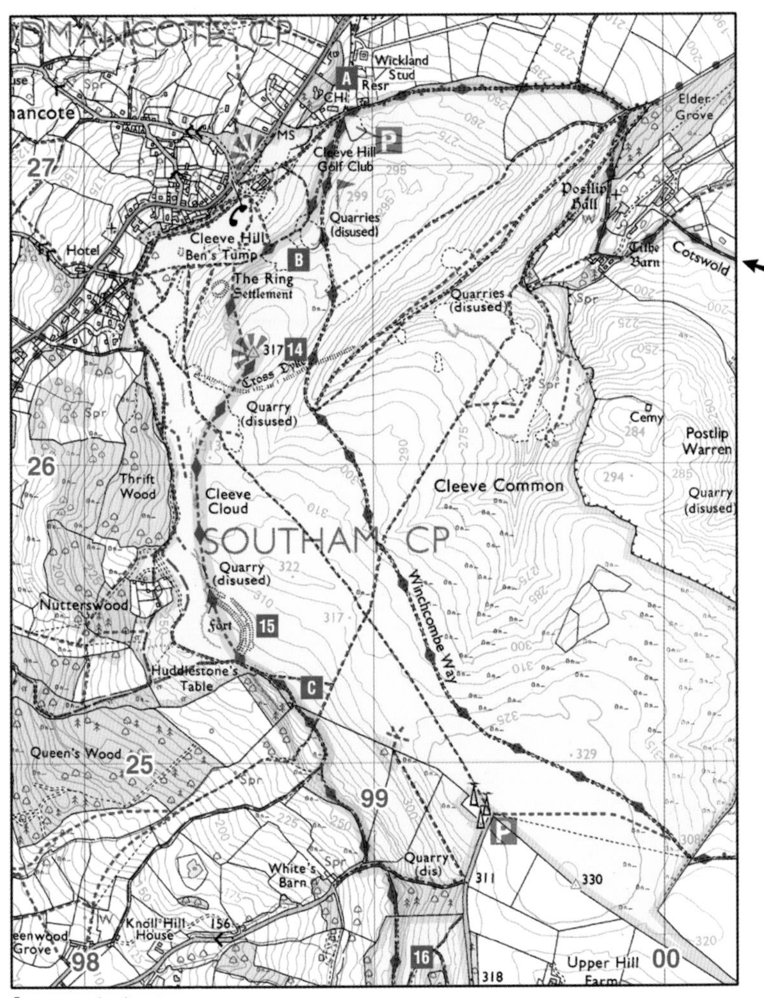

Contours are given in metres
The vertical interval is 5m

ways divide, take the lower, wide grassy track that runs along the top of the steep slope. It continues beside the fence forming the boundary to a small wood until a gate is reached **C**. Go through the gate and follow the grassy path through the field, a meadow rich with wild flowers, probably seen at its best in spring when it is a mass of cowslips. Continue on the path that heads downhill and then swings round to the left, levelling out to follow the edge of a small copse. Keep on this path, with the fence to the right. At the track junction turn left into the sunken way and at the top of a short rise turn right on to the broad track, running between fences at the edge of a beech wood.

This now enters the Bill Smyllie Nature Reserve **16**, an area of rough,

*An opportunity for walkers to pause and admire the magnificent views from the top of Cleeve Hill.*



uncultivated grassland, notable mainly for being home to more than 30 species of butterfly. Such areas have become increasingly important in modern Britain, where sadly the steady advance of modern farming and urban expansion has destroyed habitats, leading to a catastrophic fall in numbers of these beautiful, fragile creatures. Where ways divide in front of a hilltop crowned with trees, continue straight on along the path that bends round to the right towards a hanging valley. This provides a pleasant contrast to the very airy upland walking enjoyed so far on this section of the Way. Now the path is sheltered by grassy banks studded with hawthorn thickets. Leaving the valley by a small patch of woodland, the path once again emerges at the scarp edge, and again there is a view over Cheltenham. Cross a stile and take the path that winds through the gorse bushes lining the edge. This emerges by a complex of old quarry workings **D**. Turn left above the quarries, then sharp right to take the path going downhill beside the wire fence at the edge of the deep quarry.

The rough grassland has now been left behind for fields and farmland, and the track comes out at the end of a dead-end road. Turn left through the gate to take the path at the edge of the wood, the latter part of which seems like an arcade, its roof formed by the branches of the beech trees arching over the path. At the end of this path **E** turn left on to the road, still shaded by the branches. At the crossroads, turn right, and where the road turns sharply left **F** go through the gate to continue in the same direction down the green track. It is a real pleasure to see that the accompanying drystone wall has been beautifully restored, with some attractive little features: watch out for the place where it has been neatly curved to fit round a tree in the next field.

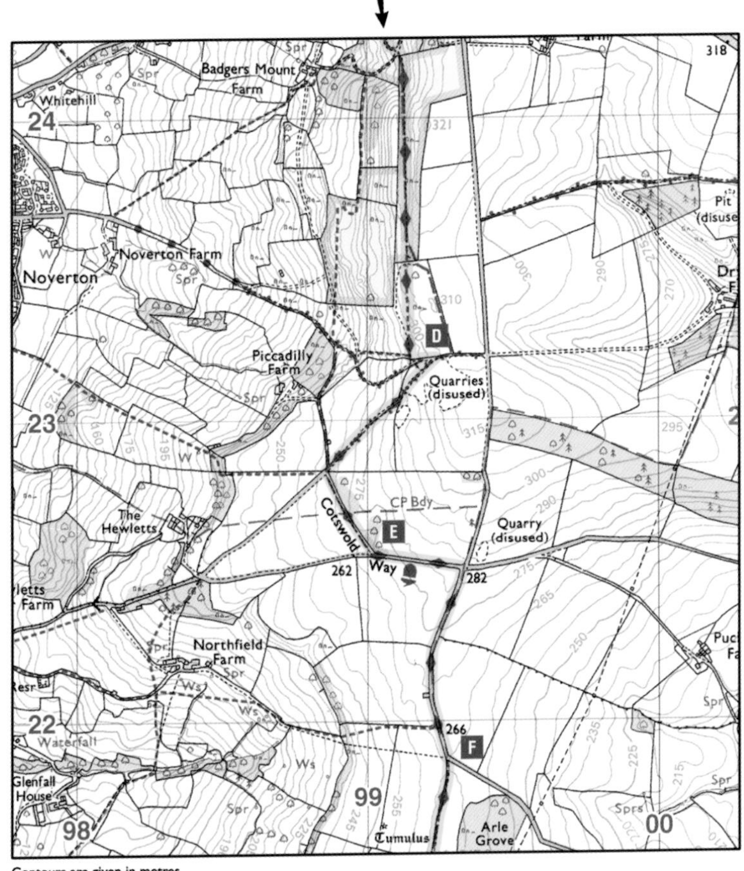


Contours are given in metres
The vertical interval is 5m

Ramsons and bluebells brighten the path through the springtime woods on the approach to Dowdeswell reservoir.

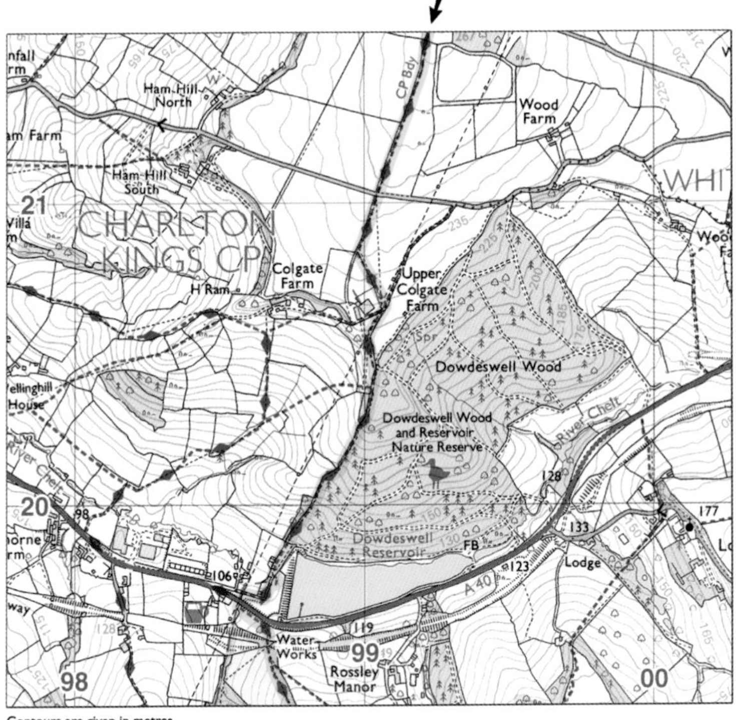


Contours are given in metres
The vertical interval is 5m

At the end of the track, cross straight over the road via two gates and continue on the path directly opposite, which leads to the extensive Dowdeswell Wood Nature Reserve. This is an area of mixed woodland, but since 1992 there has been a steady clearing of the conifers. This has allowed ground vegetation to spread, and ramsons, the wild garlic, has certainly flourished. Even those who are not very sure about plant recognition cannot fail to recognise the smell. The path goes steadily and quite steeply downhill. There is no shortage of wildlife in the wood, though you need sharp eyes to spot anything among the trees. In particular, this has become a breeding ground for the dormouse, and there is even a reminder of when this part of the country was settled by the Romans – the Roman snail, said to have been brought from Italy, not for conservation but as a delicacy; perhaps the local ramsons would have been an appropriate accompaniment. Emerging from the wood by the house, the track crosses the watercourse carrying the overflow from Dowdeswell reservoir. This is home to several species of wildfowl as well as amphibians. Crossing the watercourse, turn right then left on to the path up to the road.

## Dowdeswell Reservoir

**Originally built in 1886 by damming the headwaters of the River Chelt to provide Cheltenham with water. The water filter plant was added in the 1920s**

# 6 Dowdeswell to Leckhampton Hill

*4.7 miles (7.6 km)*

**Ascent** 902 feet (275 metres)
**Descent** 344 feet (105 metres)
**Lowest point** Dowdeswell 377 feet (115 metres)
**Highest point** 951 feet (290 metres)

Cross over the busy A40 and turn left a short walk up the road on to the roadside path. Where the road begins to turn to the left, turn right **A** on to the track. Cross the line of the old railway that once ran from Cheltenham to Banbury, a minor link in the Great Western Railway network. Nearby fenceposts are actually cut-down lengths of the distinctive GWR broad-gauge rails. The broad track swings round to the right towards Lineover Wood. From the gate take the track that heads steadily uphill. The area is managed by the Woodland Trust and little poetic messages have been put up all along the route, though you need to keep a sharp lookout, for it is very easy to miss them altogether. They are all part of Tom Clarke's work, *Twelve Pauses in Three Woods*. The other two woods are Penn and Coaley. One here in Lineover Wood, for example, reads:

*The shade of broad leaves*
*The fragrance of conifers*

And that is exactly what you get on this part of the walk, with dense conifers to one side and broadleaved trees to the other. Near the top of this long climb, the path steepens and walkers are helped on their way by a set of wooden steps.

Emerging on to an area of rough grassland, continue in the same direction, following the path beside the wood. Where the view eventually opens out to the north it is once again dominated by Cheltenham, which the Cotswold Way is gradually working its way round. Where paths divide at the edge of the next patch of woodland **B**, go through the gate and turn right to take the path through a very attractive area of broadleaved woodland, especially notable for its large-leaved lime trees. Leaving the wood brings a return to an attractive grassy hillside and a view over Old Dole Farm, with a pond and a beautiful walled garden, enclosed by high brick walls. The path now heads on the level across the face of the hill, but up ahead it can be seen all too clearly heading up at an angle, back to the top of the escarpment. This is a steep climb, but a bench at the top **17** provides a welcome opportunity to pause for a while and enjoy the view, which looks back along the route all the way to Cleeve Hill.

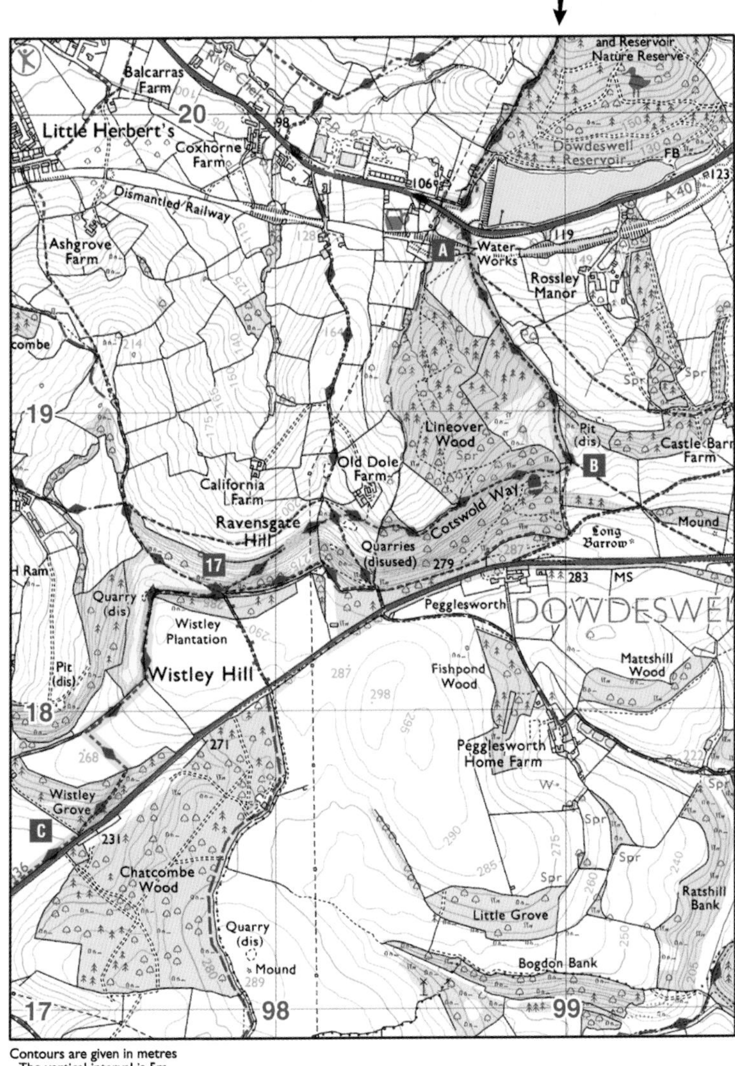

Contours are given in metres
The vertical interval is 5m

The scattered trees make ideal lookouts for hungry kestrels.

Turn right to follow the path that runs along the edge of the wood and, where that comes to an end, continue following the fence round to the left, still keeping to the escarpment edge. Look out for a gate in the fence on the left and go through it to continue in the same direction, but now on the opposite side of the hedge. This is a clearly defined path between fences that bends sharply round to the left to head towards a patch of woodland. Go into the wood and turn right, heading down towards the busy main road. At the road **C** turn right through the gate to take the field path running beside the hedge, which emerges by the busy

*The rock pinnacle known as the Devil's Chimney, left behind by quarrying, is a famous landmark on the edge of Leckhampton Hill.*





road junction at Seven Springs **D**. This was once thought to be the source of the Thames, but actually feeds the River Churn, which joins the Thames at Cricklade. Cross over via the traffic island, then turn sharp right down the minor road, passing a farm with two old wind pumps, which presumably have given it its name, Windmill Farm. As the road bends sharp left, continue straight on down the track.

Where the ways divide **E**, turn sharp left on to the footpath going slightly uphill. The path stays just inside the little wood, at the end of which it turns sharp right to emerge on to the grassland of Hartley Hill, with a thicket to the right. It meanders through a small wooded area, eventually coming completely into the open right at the escarpment edge in one of those dramatic revelations of a panoramic view that are such a feature of this walk. The route now follows the very obvious track along the edge. Where the track divides, keep to the upper level, and the path begins to swing left towards Leckhampton Hill. Here the rock faces below the summit are evidence that this was once an important area for quarrying. Many of the tracks that can be seen running across the scarp are the remains of old tramways – simple railways along which trucks filled with stone were hauled by horses. Because the gap between the rails had to be kept clear for the horses' feet, the transverse sleepers familiar from our modern railways couldn't be used. Instead the rails were mounted on parallel lines of stone blocks, some of which can still be seen in situ. Continue on towards the little patch of woodland. Where the ways divide, take the narrow path, passing to the right of the trig. point. There is now evidence of considerably more quarrying here. A dramatic reminder of those days is the isolated rock pinnacle left behind by the quarrymen and known by a romantic name: the Devil's Chimney **18**; it can be seen just below the escarpment rim.

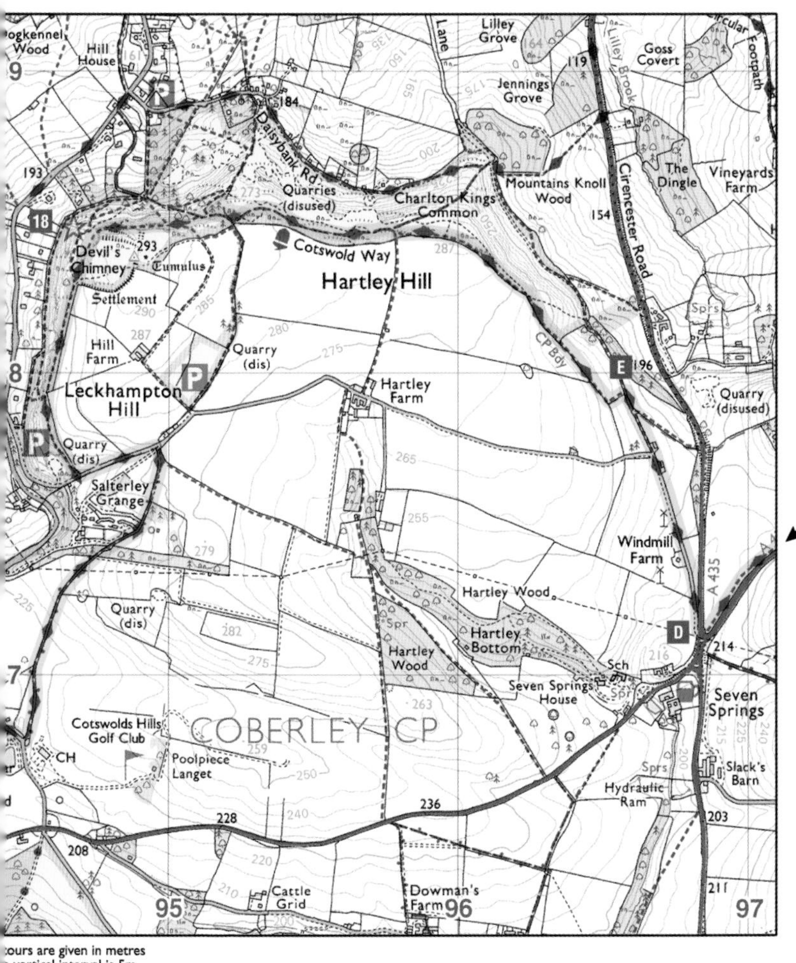

ours are given in metres
e vertical interval is 5m

# 7 Leckhampton Hill to Birdlip

*5.6 miles (9 km)*
*Parking: Quarry, Hartley Lane, grid reference SO 946176, no charge*

**Ascent** 426 feet (130 metres)
**Descent** 410 feet (125 metres)
**Lowest point** Greenway Lane 722 feet (220 metres)
**Highest point** Birdlip 951 feet (290 metres)

The route continues along the escarpment edge and passes above a considerable quarry, now used as a car park. From here, the path drops down to the road **A**. Turn left up this quiet country lane, through a mixed landscape of arable farmland and rougher grassland, studded with mature trees. At the top of the short hill, turn right on to a broad track, bordered by a tall hedge on the right. Over to the left, there is a wide expanse of typically open, rather windswept, Cotswold plateau. A very stony path now leads gently downhill, passing through a band of mixed woodland to emerge rather surprisingly at a modern housing complex. Beyond that is an area of meadows, enlivened with trees and flowers, flourishing from the protection afforded by the lower slopes of the hills. This gives way, not for the first or last time along the route, to a golf course. The path ends at the roadway **B**. Turn right, passing the old Ullenwood Manor, now home to the National Star Centre, a college for young people with physical disabilities. The surrounding land is protected by a gargantuan windbreak of tall, closely packed conifers. At the crossroads, continue straight on along the road marked as a dead end. The view to the left is still blocked by high hedges, but to the right there is a lovely prospect, across meadows towards Leckhampton Hill. That view too is briefly lost, but is replaced by an attractive little wood, with a variety of broadleaved trees. An old army camp on the left was once used as a firefighters' training ground. Beyond that, the road enters a woodland area. Ignore the first track by a gate and go a little way downhill to a flight of wooden steps on the left **C**.

The steps lead up to a path on the edge of the wood, where the escarpment sweeps round in a gentle curve, emphasised by the tall trees. Over to the left, a hump bristling with conifers can be glimpsed through a screen of trees. This is Crippets Neolithic long barrow **19**, not nearly as spectacular and well preserved as Belas Knap. This is an attractive woodland walk, enlivened by the views whenever there is a break in the trees. Having spent many miles walking with a view of Cheltenham, this offers a sighting of Gloucester,

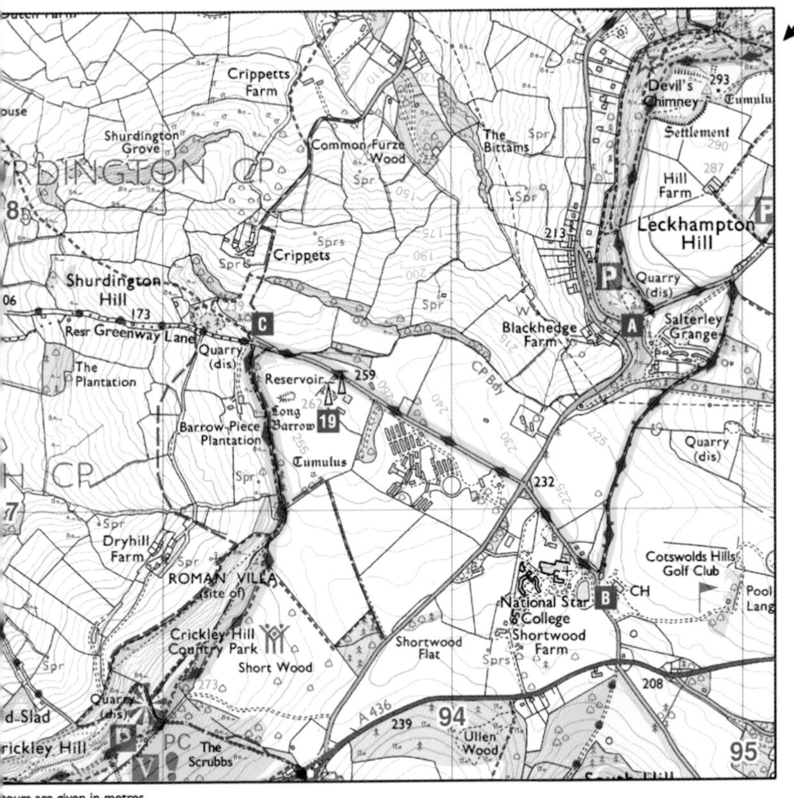


tours are given in metres
e vertical interval is 5m

dominated by the cathedral, with its magnificent central tower rising to a height of 225 feet (60 metres). Closer at hand, you look down on Dryhill Farm, which paradoxically boasts a pond as its main feature and lies next to springs. Perhaps the original owner had a sense of irony.

The path arrives at a stile giving access to the conservation land of Crickley Hill. Stay on the path, with the fence on the left, and where tracks divide carry straight on. Every time there is a break in the trees, a magnificent view opens up, but it is mainly the woodland itself that makes this part of the walk so enjoyable. The path meanders through an area of coppiced trees before giving way to more mature trees. The old drystone boundary wall has been beautifully restored. Where paths cross, go through the gate on the right and carry on down to the edge of the escarpment, where the views that have been fleetingly enjoyed along the way can now be fully taken in. The broad panorama is still dominated by the tower of Gloucester Cathedral, but also includes the rather less appealing M5. This is a popular spot, served by big car parks. Head off to the right

*The panoramic view from the escarpment at The Peak.*



from the visitor centre towards a panorama table and picnic bench. Theoretically, the view extends all the way to the Blorenge, which rises above the Usk valley near Abergavenny on the edge of the Black Mountains. Even if this claim suggests an optimistic view of the British climate, this is still a place to stop and admire the scenery. There is also a great deal of interest nearer to hand. This is yet another Iron Age promontory fort **20**.

The walk continues up to the wall that closes off the end of the promontory. Turn left through the gate to follow the track by the edge. This is an area of humps and hollows from old quarries. The route sticks close to the wall and offers beautiful walking on springy turf, the experience only slightly marred by the increasing noise of traffic as it grinds uphill on the nearby road. Enter the woodland, keeping to the broad track, still following the line of the scarp. This is mature woodland, notable for some splendid beech. Where tracks divide keep to the right, still staying close to the edge. A gate leads to a path just above the busy road, and from here a wide grassy track stays close to the fence. In the clearing, head towards the wooden gate in front of the buildings, then take the gate on the right, finally emerging on the roadside **D**. Cross over this very busy road by the traffic island, then turn right up the footpath beside The Air Balloon pub. Immediately beyond the phone box, the path turns off from the road towards the wood.

Go through a gap in the fence by the post to take the path into the wood, and the sounds of traffic soon become mercifully muffled. Where tracks divide, turn up to the left on the narrow path, which brings you once again to the escarpment edge, then dips down below the car park and viewpoint. The name of the site, Barrow Wake, is also a clue to an important archaeological find. The barrow **21**, now lost under the road, was a Bronze Age round barrow, or burial mound. Quarry-workers unearthed three skeletons, one of which was of a woman who had a beautiful bronze mirror entombed with her. Known as the Birdlip Mirror, it is now in Gloucester museum. Having curved down below the car park, the path now climbs steeply back up to the edge, and there are views back to the quarry faces that line the edge of Crickley Hill.

Although the path keeps to the edge, it is very much a switchback affair, but it gives splendid views, not just down into the Severn Vale but also back along the escarpment to the earlier part of the walk. At the end of this open section, go through the gate into the woodland and turn right, still keeping close to the edge of the wood. This provides the best of both worlds: the pleasures of mature woodland and open vistas. The path leads to the end of the next promontory, known simply as The Peak **E**. Turn sharp left to pass along the opposite side of the promontory; after passing a high quarry face, the route arrives at the Birdlip road.

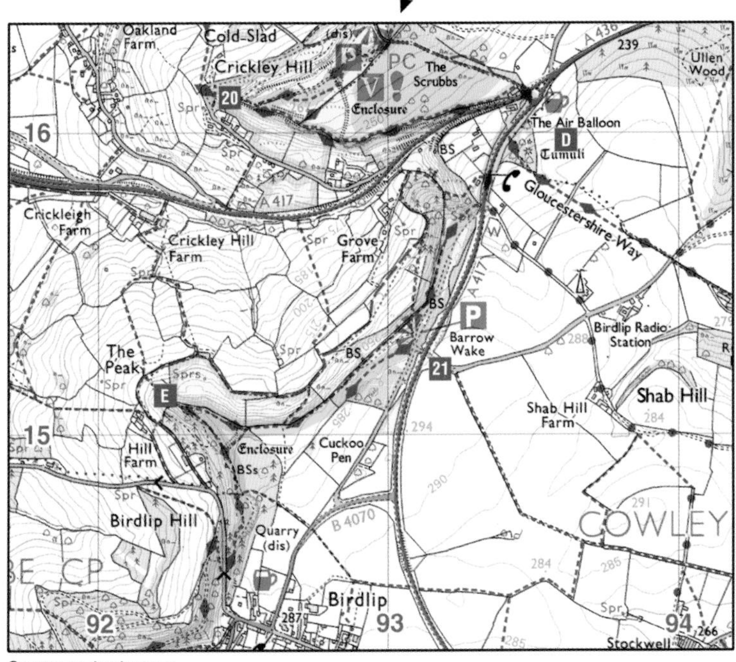


Contours are given in metres
The vertical interval is 5m

*Crinkley Hill. The rampart of the promontory fort can be clearly seen, running at right angles to the escarpment edge.*

## Crickley Hill fort

Crickley Hill has all the characteristics of this type of fortress, with a main rampart, which at its highest rises 9 feet (3 metres), accompanied by a ditch, which excavation revealed to be 8 feet (2.5 metres) deep. The steep slope is now even less accessible than it would have been 2,000 years ago, as quarrying has created sheer rock faces.

This is a formidable defence, but there is a bit of a mystery: a second set of lesser ramparts can be seen closer to the point, further to the west. But this is not the end of the story. When archaeologists began investigating the site in the 1960s, they discovered that the timescale had to be moved back to around 4000 BC, for they discovered that the lesser earthworks were the

remains of a Neolithic causewayed camp. The story they unearthed was a dramatic one: a huge number of arrowheads were discovered and the buildings within the camp appear to have been burned to the ground as the result of a battle fought here around 3450 BC. There was some evidence of activity in the Bronze Age, but the next major settlement was that by the Iron Age people whose work first catches the eye, and who probably arrived around the 7th century BC. The settlement continued after the end of the Roman occupation, with some evidence of a Dark Ages hamlet on the site. After that the hill was used for grazing and quarried for stone until modern times. It is extraordinary to think that so many changes have come to this one small promontory on the edge of the Cotswold escarpment.

# 8 Birdlip to Painswick

*8.6 miles (13.9 km)*
*Parking: Barrow Wake, grid reference SO 931154, no charge*

**Ascent** 590 feet (180 metres)
**Descent** 1,066 feet (325 metres)
**Lowest point** Paiinswick 476 feet (145 metres)
**Highest point** Birdlip 951 feet (290 metres)

The village of Birdlip itself is just a short walk up the road to the left, but the Way crosses straight over to continue into the woods **A**. Although the village now stands on a minor road, the site is actually right on the line of Roman Ermin Way, which ran from Gloucester to Silchester. Immediately on leaving the road, turn sharp right to take the path that heads downhill through the trees. It is an encouraging sign to see so many

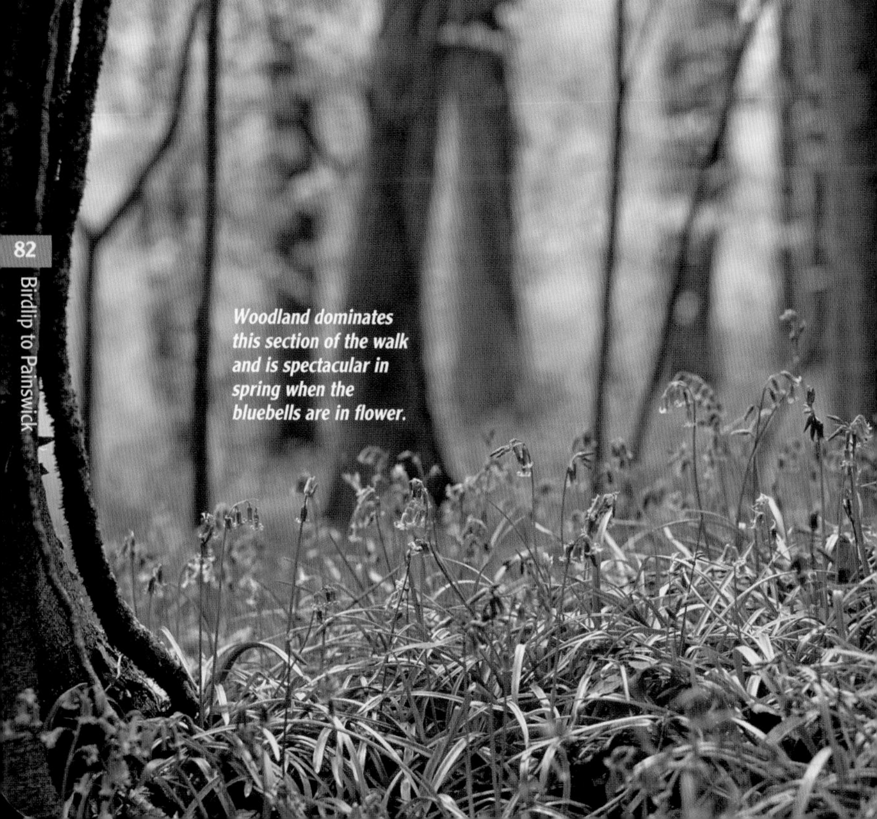
*Woodland dominates this section of the walk and is spectacular in spring when the bluebells are in flower.*

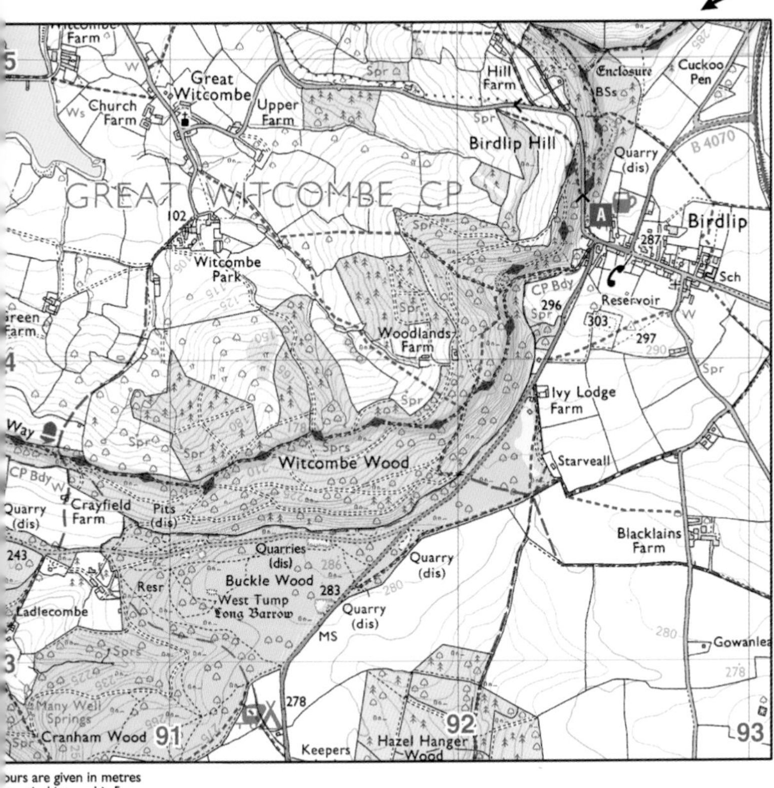


ours are given in metres
vertical interval is 5m

saplings in this part of the wood, ensuring growth for the future. At the foot of the hill turn sharp left on to the track at the edge of the wood, and where tracks divide take the path to the left going gently uphill again. Woodland will dominate the walk for the next few miles. There is wildlife in plenty in the woods, but it is seldom seen. There is, however, a lot to listen out for. Songbirds include the wood warbler, notable for a controlled vibrato that would be the envy of any operatic soprano, and the chaffinch, which is unusual in not having any one distinctive song. Other unmistakable sounds are the rattle of the woodpecker and the harsh call of the pheasant. There are deer in the woods, but they are shy and elusive. Wild garlic is prolific and, especially after rain, the smell can be almost overpowering. There are also patches of pendulous sedge, which get their name from the way the spikes begin to droop at the beginning of summer.

The track swings round to the left in a little hollow way and meets a broader track where it turns right. There is exposed rock underfoot, with occasional fossil shells to be seen – a reminder that this rock at the top of the hill once formed the bed of a sea. Where tracks cross by an old quarry face, carry straight on and continue on the same level route at the next track junction. The track now heads downhill, with a patch of conifer to the right. At the track division, turn left, going slightly uphill to join the wall that marks the boundary of Witcombe Park. There was once a grand entrance to the park from the woods, but all that remains are the two imposing gateposts. Reaching a clearing, turn sharp right and a view opens up, this time down to the Witcombe reservoirs. Keep to this broad track, ignoring the various turnings. Where tracks divide, take the one on the left heading uphill, which once again emerges by the edge. The path to the right leads down to Great Witcombe Roman Villa **22**. A little further on, you can look down on the villa, though trees may obscure the view in summer. This is arguably the best way to see this site, because it is spread out before you like an architect's plan. Here are the main house and the outbuildings, all set out round an enclosed courtyard. This woodland section ends where the track emerges beside modern houses.

Cooper's Hill is only a hamlet, but it boasts a charming little cottage, The Haven, which has been offering refreshments to walkers on the Cotswold Way for many years. Apart from the temptations of a pot of tea, it offers a lovely spot to sit and admire the view before tackling the next big climb. Carry on down the road to the cluster of houses and where the road divides turn left, then immediately left again on to the footpath at the bottom of the steep, grassy hill **23**.

## Cheese Rolling

It is here, at Cooper's Hill, on Spring Bank Holiday Mondays, that the annual cheese rolling competition takes place. It is basically a very simple competition: a whole cheese is sent bowling down the hill and the racers pursue it, running, tumbling and sliding down the hill. It was originally part of a midsummer festival known as the Cooper's Hill Wake, which when first recorded in the early 1800s included other sports, from bobbing for apples to shin-kicking contests. Other aspects that have been retained include the scattering of sweets for children at the top of the hill, a ceremony thought to have survived from old fertility rites to encourage a rich harvest.

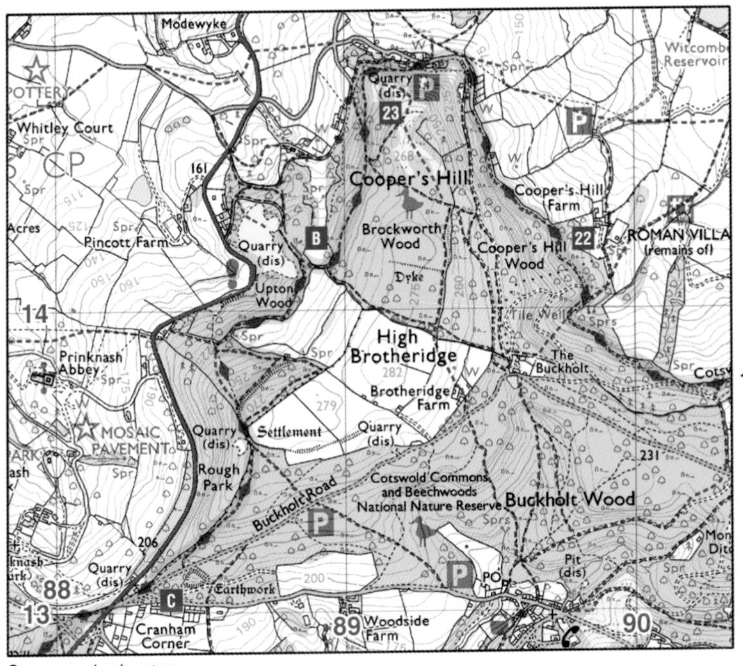

Contours are given in metres
The vertical interval is 5m

Go through the kissing-gate into the Cooper's Hill Nature Reserve, once again back in mature woodland. After a steep little climb, take the path round to the left and then turn left again, still going uphill. At the top of the hill is the maypole, which marks the starting point for the annual cheese rolling. If the idea of running down this hill seemed daunting when standing at the bottom looking up, then viewed from here looking down it is simply terrifying. At the maypole turn right on to the level track; this swings round to the right into Brockworth Wood, which offers woodland walking at its best. Here you find a rich variety of mature trees, with little glades dappled by sunlight filtering through them. Like many woods, however, these have a complex web of paths and tracks, so care must be taken to follow the instructions and keep an eye out for waymarkers. The track goes back downhill, and at the foot of the slope turns sharp left. At the track division take the route to the right and at the gate **B** turn left on to the track beside the field. Reaching the edge of the wood again, the track turns round to the right. This is an area which was once coppiced to provide wood for charcoal burners. Ignore the steps to the right and keep straight on. There is a long, steady climb with a boundary wall to the right of the path. At the top of the hill turn right and where ways divide by a noticeboard giving details of Buckholt Wood, a National Nature Reserve, take the track to the right which now goes back downhill again to reach the road **C**.

At the road turn right to its junction with the main road. Cross over on to a footpath almost immediately opposite, which plunges once more into the woods. Follow the line of the stone wall, then after a short way leave the line of the wall for the path going off to the left. Cross straight over the next road and take the lower track on the left. Arriving at yet another road, turn right and, just beyond the large house on the left, take the track on through the gate to reach the open grassland of Painswick Hill. Almost immediately, turn left off the broad track for the bridleway leading out on to the golf course. The next part of the route is reassuringly easy to follow and can be seen heading away to pass just below the ramparts of Painswick Beacon **24**. This is the most imposing Iron Age fort met so far, with earthworks surrounding nearly the whole of the hilltop. The defences consist of double and even treble banks and ditches, and the entrance to the north-west is inturned. The interior has been damaged first by quarrying then by the construction of the golf course, but it still remains a very impressive monument. Just past the end of the fortifications, the path passes a deep quarry.

*Painswick Post Office.*



At the road turn left and where the road turns away downhill turn right to return to another footpath. The path now goes to the left of the iron gates giving access to an old quarry. To the left, the land falls away steeply down a heavily wooded slope. Coming back out into the open, take the path that runs above the wall surrounding the cemetery **D**, cross the road and continue on the grassy path over the far end of the golf course and through the walkers' car park. At the roadway turn right towards a curious octagonal building in the distance. At the road junction turn left into Painswick

The route passes the former Gyde's Orphanage, founded by a Victorian businessman, and then carries on down Gloucester Street. At the end of the road, turn right towards the church. Like so many towns and villages in the region, Painswick grew wealthy on wool, and the wealth shows. There are a number of very fine houses, and one real curiosity: the post office on the main road. This looks like two tiny buildings stuck together, one timber-framed, the other of stone, holding each other up like a pair of drunks as they lean at odd angles. Originally built as a private house in 1478, the post office had its moment of glory when it was chosen as one of four to be featured on stamps issued in 1997 to

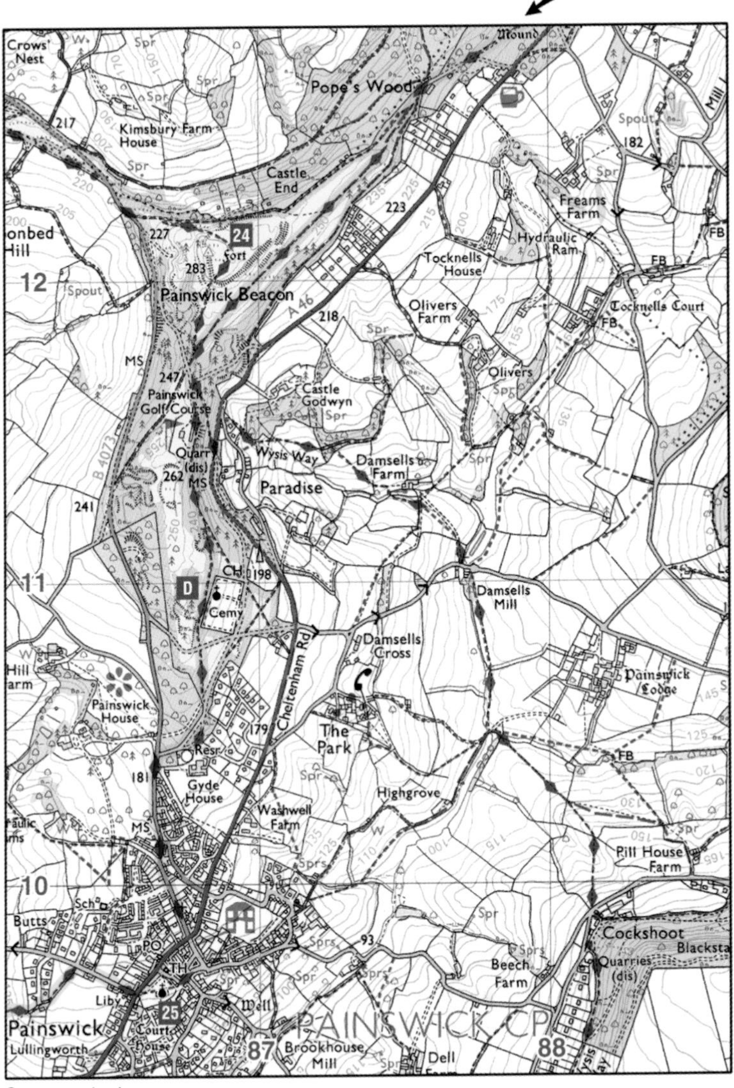


Contours are given in metres
The vertical interval is 5m

celebrate the centenary of the National Association of Sub-Postmasters.

Painswick's chief claim to fame is the churchyard **25**. At the entrance are the village stocks, an oddity in that the miscreants' legs were held in iron hoops. The churchyard contains perhaps the finest set of carved table tombs in Britain, around which are 99 yews. The church, which would be memorable elsewhere, seems almost disappointing in such a setting, having been much restored over the centuries. It does, however, have its own oddity: a massive model of Drake's flagship, the *Bonaventure*.

# 9 Painswick to King's Stanley

*7.8 miles (12.6 km)*
*Parking: walkers' car park, grid reference SO 868105, no charge*

**Ascent** 1,033 feet (315 metres)
**Descent** 1,082 feet (330 metres)
**Lowest point** King's Stanley 82 feet (25 metres)
**Highest point** Shortwood 771 feet (235 metres)

Leave Painswick by Edge Road, which turns right off the main road, opposite the lych-gate at the entrance to the churchyard. The road leads past yet more handsome stone houses, with yew trees to rival those of the church. Immediately beyond these **A** turn left through a kissing-gate to take the path at the edge of the field, which leads to a second gate and a little lane between the houses. Arriving at the road, turn left down an even narrower path beside the houses. Emerging from the lane, a fine view opens out once again. Keep close to the fence on the right and head towards Painswick Rugby Club. Just past the tennis courts, turn diagonally right by the gate towards a marker that can be seen just in front of the patch of woodland. Follow the track with the hedge to the right and go through the gate to take the path alongside the wood. This arrives at Washbrook Farm **26**, which boasts some elaborate carving and the date 1691 over the door. The building has had a very varied history, having been used both as a grain mill and fulling mill in its time, and has clearly seen much alteration, since it now appears to have a fireplace on an outside wall.

Cross over the drive and take the lane to the left, passing the outbuildings. A broad track climbs the hill, and looking back you can see that Washbrook Farm is bigger than it appeared, rising a full three storeys. After about 100 yards, leave this track by the gate on the left and the path briefly penetrates an area of mature woodland before crossing a small stream on a footbridge. Climb up to the next gate and turn left, following the edge of the wood towards a milestone, which carries the news that you are now 55 miles from Bath – very nearly halfway there, which is encouraging.

From here the path runs past the prominent clump of trees to a gate in the fence. Cross the track and turn left; looking back there is a good view of the Painswick valley, with the church spire still a prominent landmark. Stone steps go up to the road leading to The Edgemoor Inn. Turn right on to the road, which is the main route between Stroud and Gloucester and carries a lot of traffic. Opposite the pub **B** cross the road, go through the gate and bear right on to the common. This has a rich variety of wild flowers, from spring right through summer.

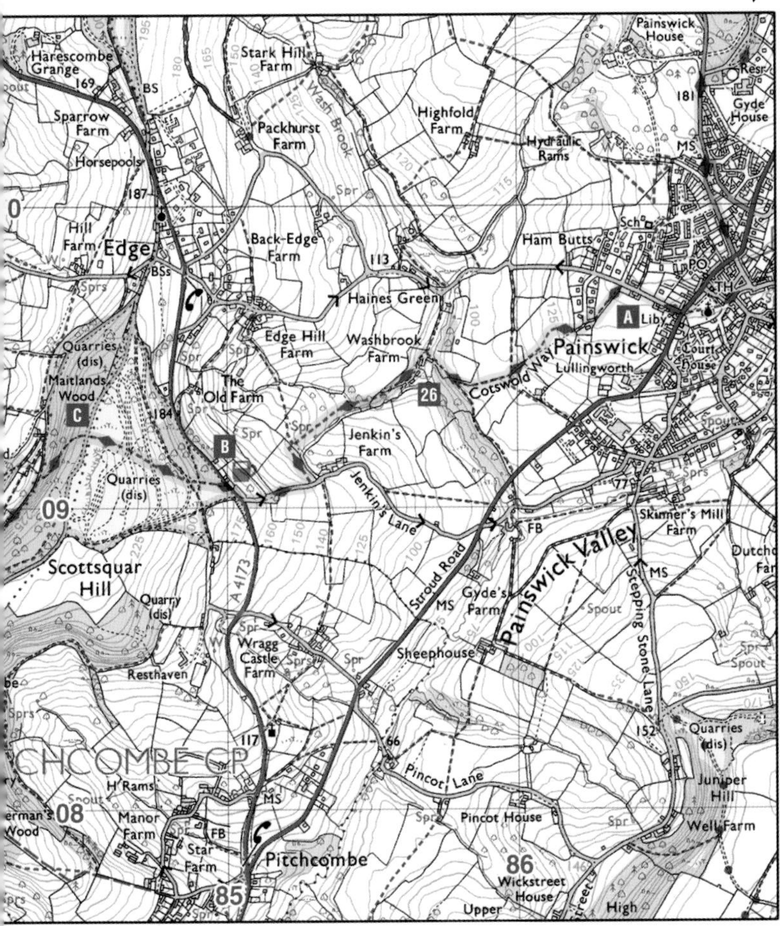


tours are given in metres
e vertical interval is 5m

The route now enters an area much disturbed by quarrying. Cross over the broad track and continue straight up the hill to fringe woodland of oak and silver birch. Reaching another small path, turn left, still heading uphill, and continue in this direction, ignoring the various tracks that cross the route. The tussock grass is home to a variety of orchids – over the years six different species have been found here. The way is marked by posts, and at the end of this section turn left towards a quarry face and take the steps down to the road.

Go straight over to take the track leading into the woods. This is a typical beechwood hanger, which echoes with the mewing cries of circling buzzards. Where the path immediately divides **C**, carry straight on. This is another attractive woodland walk, at the end of which the track turns left and the view opens out to the River Severn. Take the broad track that serves a sprinkling of houses, still staying close to the escarpment edge. This continues, leading back into the wood. The path appears to be closed by a wooden barrier, but that is only there to keep out vehicles, and walkers continue straight on past it. To the right are the remains of an old forest boundary wall.

**Laurie Lee**

**Stroud, a short distance from the Cotswold Way, was the birthplace of the author, though the family soon moved to nearby Slad, which is where he drank cider with Rosie. He returned to the village later in life, and there is now a memorial window to him in the church.**

At the road, turn right. This is a very quiet road, which leads to the Cliff Well and Cliffwell Cottages. Just before the road starts to go steeply downhill **D**, turn left on to the track by the stone house. The path is now back in woodland and soon reaches a large inscribed stone, known as the Cromwell Stone, which commemorates the raising of the siege of Gloucester in the Civil War, but is now virtually illegible. Occasionally the woods clear on the right to give views down to the Severn Vale, but in general this is a very attractive woodland walk on a good path that stays close to the escarpment edge. The appearance of houses again marks the arrival at a road: turn left and almost immediately right through the gate by the stables to take the path to Haresfield Beacon. Reaching an area of open grassland, take the path with the fence on the left. Go through the gate to continue in the same direction on the opposite side of the fence, then turn left to head towards the trig. point **27**. From here, there is a wide view down over the Severn Vale, with the Cotswold escarpment receding away into the distance.

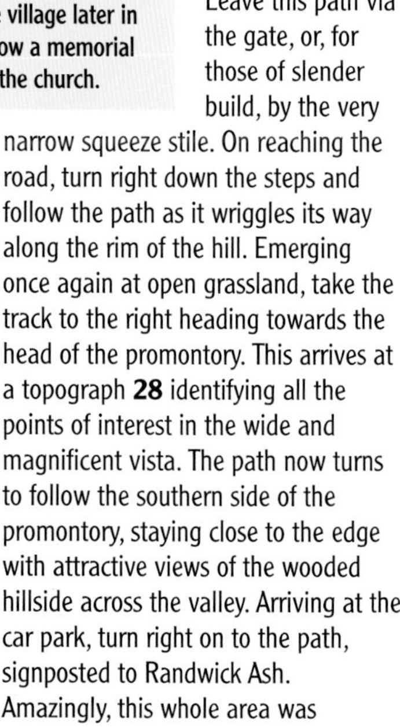

From the trig. point, turn sharp left to take the undulating path on the opposite side of the promontory. Leave the grassy area by the gate to take the narrow path that winds its way along the side of a fence before entering an area of scrubby woodland. Leave this path via the gate, or, for those of slender build, by the very narrow squeeze stile. On reaching the road, turn right down the steps and follow the path as it wriggles its way along the rim of the hill. Emerging once again at open grassland, take the track to the right heading towards the head of the promontory. This arrives at a topograph **28** identifying all the points of interest in the wide and magnificent vista. The path now turns to follow the southern side of the promontory, staying close to the edge with attractive views of the wooded hillside across the valley. Arriving at the car park, turn right on to the path, signposted to Randwick Ash. Amazingly, this whole area was earmarked for development in the

1930s, but thanks to a vigorous local protest the plans were dropped and the area was secured by the National Trust.

The Way now passes once again into woodland, offering easy walking on a broad track that follows the line of the escarpment. Most of the trees are comparatively young, large areas having been cleared for the thwarted development, but the wood is slowly returning to its full majesty. Entering an area of mixed woodland for a change, the track arrives at a gate **E**. Turn right and the track now leads past old quarries to the edge of the wood. Leave the wood by the gate and take the path down the field, with the hedge and wall on the

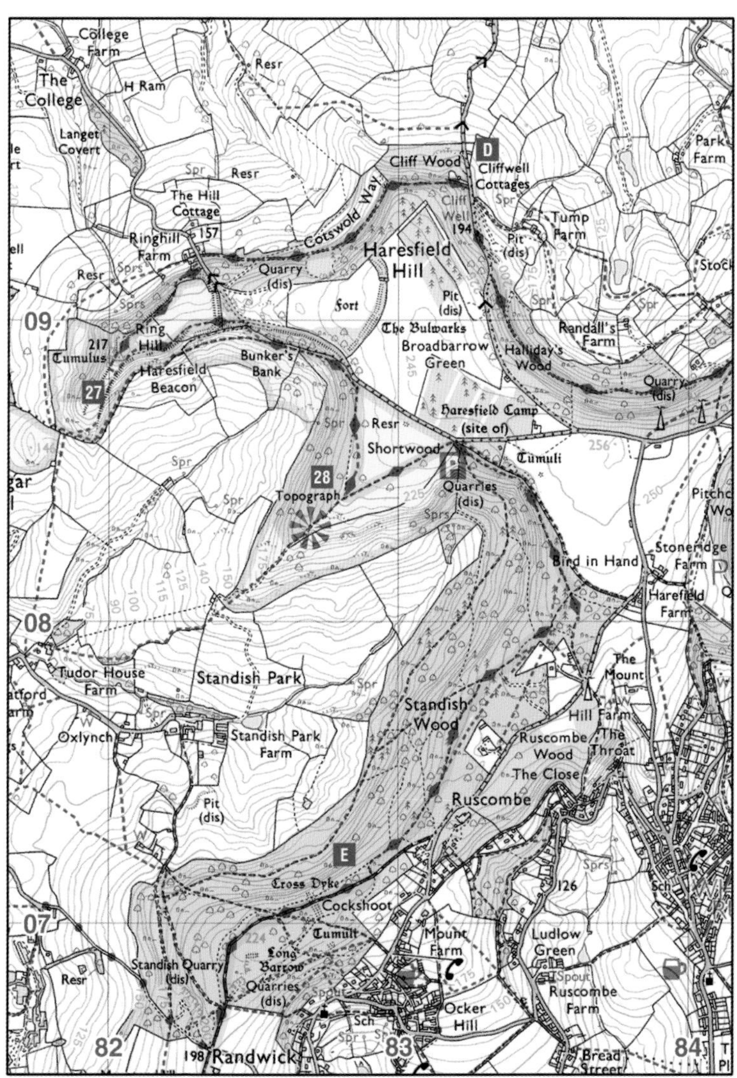

Contours are given in metres
The vertical interval is 5m

A stone stile set into a dry stone wall, with accompanying signpost pointing the way down to the Stroud valley.

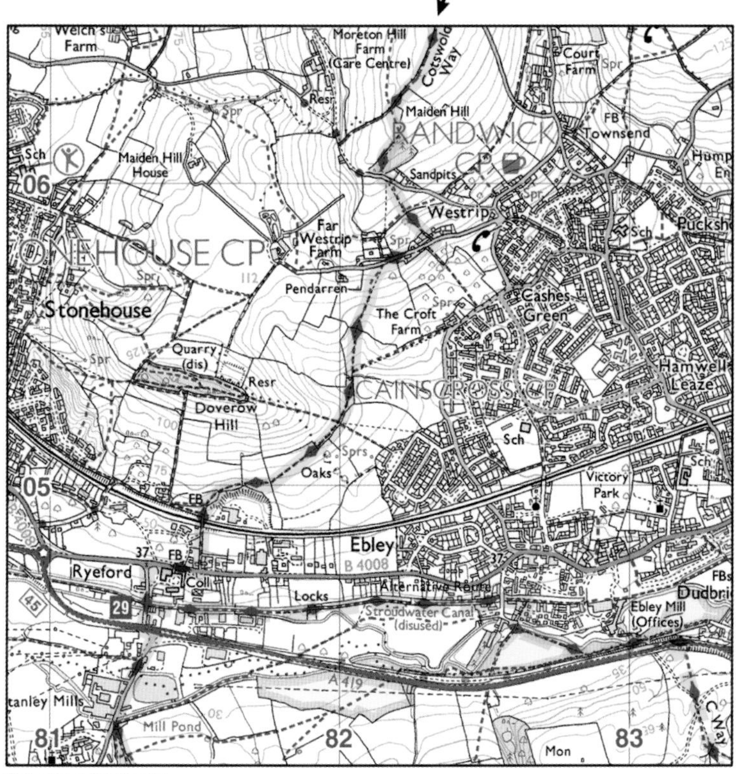

Contours are given in metres
The vertical interval is 5m

right. The view of the Stroud valley opens up, dominated by Ebley Mill, one of the survivors of the many woollen mills that once dominated the whole area. At the far side of the field continue down the farm track, then turn left opposite the gate to head for a patch of woodland. Cross the stone stile – with its adjoining 'dog stile' – and go straight down through the wood to the road. Turn left, then immediately right, to continue downhill on the obvious path to a gap between the houses. Turn right along the road, ignore the first stile and carry on to the end of the houses. Turn left across a stone stile and continue downhill towards a gate by a stand of trees. Continue across the fields and, where the walk begins to rise again, turn right by the hedge and look out for a metal squeeze stile. Once through the stile continue on to the next stile and then turn away from the field edge towards an obvious gap by a bushy tree. The route now goes round a high steel fence to arrive at a bridge across the railway, still in use between Cheltenham and London. Pass the edge of the school playing fields to arrive at the main road.

Turn right, then left by the mini roundabout, down Ryeford Road. Arriving at the bridge across the Stroudwater Canal **29**, there is now a choice of routes, which will be described in the next section.

# 10 King's Stanley to Dursley

*7.2 miles (11.6 km)*

***The two options have equal status: the first, more direct, route will be described first and the alternative will appear at the end of this section on page 100.***

**Ascent** 771 feet (235 metres)

**Descent** 951 feet (290 metres)

**Lowest point** Stanley Mill 82 feet (25 metres)

**Highest point** Coaley Peak 771 feet (235 metres)

Continue straight up the road across the canal to the busy Ebley bypass. Cross at the lights, and go down the road opposite to pass Stanley Mill **30**. This imposing building mainly dates from 1813, but it stands on a site where mills have been recorded since the middle of the 11th century. Built of brick, it contrasts with the many stone mill buildings in the area, but there is a simple explanation: the nearby town of Stonehouse had a flourishing brickworks in the 19th century. It is a handsome structure with a number of architectural flourishes, including Venetian windows. It is a very early example of a fireproof building, with cast-iron pillars supporting floors laid on brick arches. Those who are lucky enough to be here on one of the rare open days will find it a fascinating place, with a surprisingly ornate interior. Across the road one can still see the mill pond and the sluices that controlled the flow of water to the mill in its earliest working days.

Immediately beyond the mill, turn left on to the footpath, an obvious grassy track running above the modern houses of King's Stanley. At the end of the broad track, go through the gate to take the path that circles round the back of Manor Farm. Do not cross the footbridge, unless you want access to the village, but turn left past some imposing weeping willows. At the next gate turn left, then leave the farm road to take the path straight across the middle of the field. Continue along the next field with the hedge on the right and follow the field edge round the houses of Middleyard. At the end of the houses, turn right and leave the field by the little stile. The route passes the severely classical Baptist Church, which, although it carries the inscription 'Founded 1640', was actually built in 1824.

Turn left at the road, and where that begins to swing sharply to the left, cross over to take the track up beside Rosebank Cottage **A**. Just before reaching a small, timber-clad building, turn right on to the track heading up the hill. This narrow, tree-shaded path leads up to a stile to the right of the houses. Beyond that, a fine view opens out over the valley. Leave the field by the stile on the left and almost immediately turn off the road to take

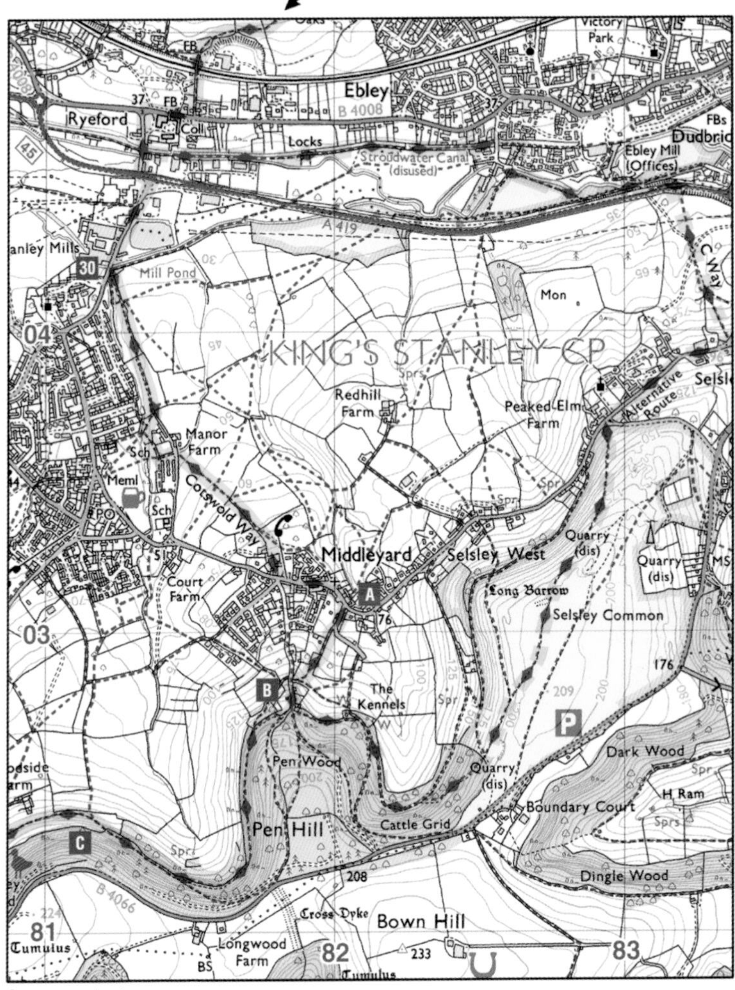

Contours are given in metres
The vertical interval is 5m

the narrow, very stony path that leads right up to the brow of the hill, where it meets a broad woodland path **B**. The other route rejoins the Way at this point.

Turn right to take this very attractive path through the trees. It comes as no surprise to find a typical escarpment wood, dominated by beech. It is all very peaceful and the only harsh noises likely to be heard are the raucous squawks of jays and the rattle of woodpeckers. The path stays close to the escarpment rim at first, but where tracks divide take the right-hand route heading downhill **C**. It arrives at the edge of the wood, offering a brief view down to the Severn, before turning back uphill to return to the trees. For a time the path stays close to the edge of the wood and breaks in the trees give views out over the Severn Vale. After the brief excursion into the open, the path sets off on a long, steady climb through the trees. It crosses a prominent broad track, still heading uphill until the escarpment edge is reached. The path now winds along the rim, the woodland falling away steeply to one side. At a track junction keep to the right; it now comes as something of a surprise to hear traffic again as the path comes up to the road. Turn right and leave the woodland by the gate to take the path on the right, which emerges at a wide expanse of grassland, waymarked by posts.

The path heads towards an obvious mound **31**. This is Nympsfield long barrow, which dates back to the New Stone Age. It was restored in 1976, to display a forecourt with a 'horned' entrance, and chambers that would once have been covered. Excavation revealed the remains of numerous people, as well as pig remains. The people all had very bad teeth, though there is no obvious explanation, unless they had damaged them trying to chew crackling. The route continues across the grassland to the popular picnic area of Coaley Peak and a magnificent panoramic view. Points of interest are shown on a display, though one will be lucky to see everything that is mentioned. On a good day, however, the view will certainly include the unmistakable conical hill known as the Sugar Loaf, which rises far away in Wales above the town of Abergavenny. In summer, this is a very popular spot, much used by hang-gliders. Take the path beside the fence to the gate which leads to a flight of steps, after which the path continues to wind round the edge of the hill. Returning to the woodland brings a dramatic landscape, with old quarry faces now overhung by creepers, creating a very jungly effect. Eventually, a flight of steps leads back up to the road. Anyone wishing to visit the well-known long barrow Hetty Pegler's Tump will have to walk down the road at this point and then retrace their steps, as there is no direct access from the Trail.

Take the slip road up towards the main road, but just before reaching it turn right on to the bridleway, heading quite steeply downhill. Where the track divides, turn left; having come rather a long way downhill, it is now time to head back up again. The path eventually levels out, and where tracks cross take the path up to the left. This is another quiet, undulating woodland walk, which again passes a large quarry face. This section ends at a clearing very close to the road. Ignore the first turning downhill and cross over to a bench to take the path on the right, heading very steeply downhill **D**. The path starts beside the rampart of

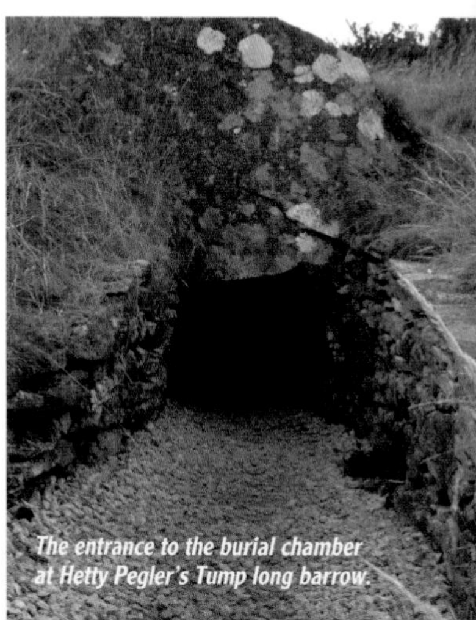
*The entrance to the burial chamber at Hetty Pegler's Tump long barrow.*

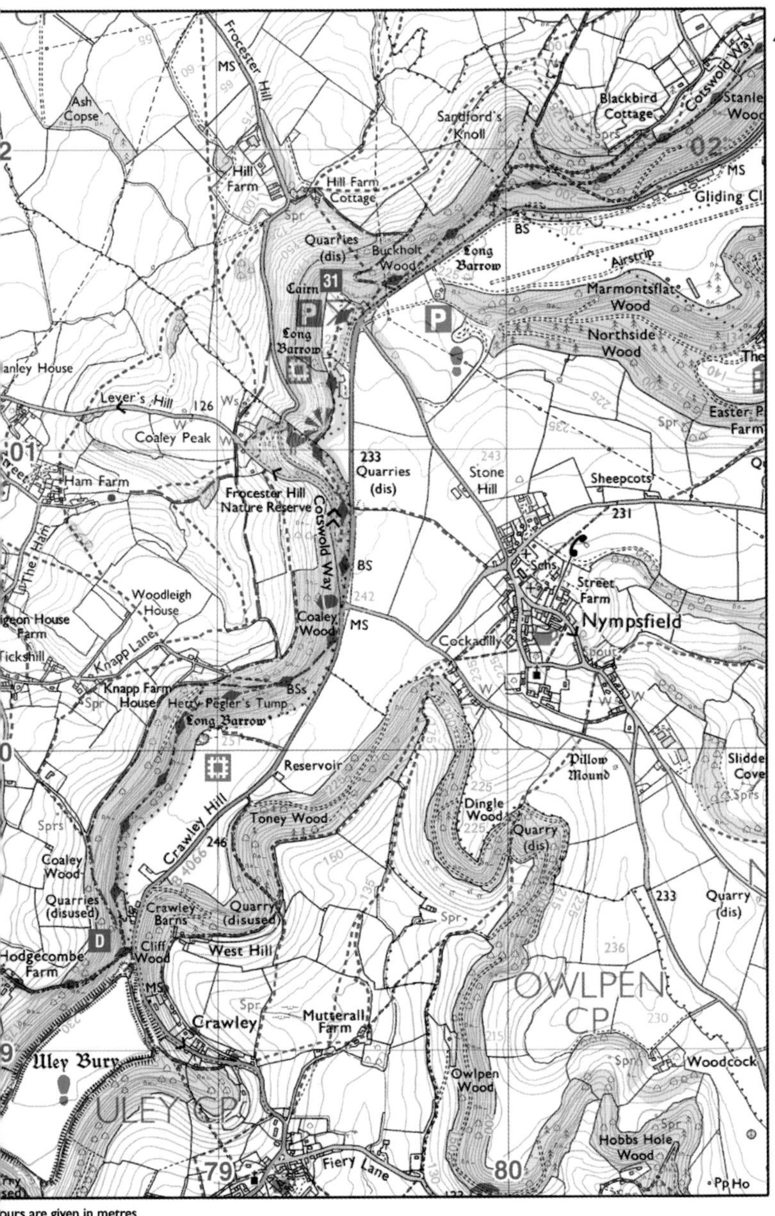


ours are given in metres
vertical interval is 5m

the impressive Uleybury hill fort, which merits a short diversion. It covers the whole promontory, enclosing an area of 32 acres (13 hectares) by means of double banks and ditches.

The path has been given a surface of loose chippings, a welcome addition to what would otherwise have been a very slippery descent in wet weather. As the path goes further downhill, it becomes a

*Looking east towards the Cotswold escarpment from Cam Long Down.*

deep sunken lane, with massive tree roots exposed in the banks at the side. The path levels out and emerges into the open, with the next objective, Cam Long Down, the most obvious feature in the landscape. Continue straight on past the farm to take the obvious track between the fields. On reaching the road, turn right and, where the road turns sharp right by the barns, cross the stile to head up the hill. The path has marker posts, but basically just goes straight up the hill in an increasingly steep climb. Carry on through the bracken near the summit to go through a gate set among the trees. The path carries on for a short way to emerge at the top of the hill. The route now is a little indistinct, but it is easy to follow: just stay on top of the ridge heading for the far end of the hill. This is much disturbed ground, bearing the humps and hollows of old quarry-workings, but the walking is superb on close-cropped grass. The views are as good as any along the whole route, and make the slog up the hill well worth the effort.

Where the path dips down briefly **E**, at a point where several tracks meet, turn left on to the broad path leading down off the hill. Where the path levels out, turn right beside the fence and after a short way turn left over a stile to take the path across the field. The Way has now returned to grazing land. Continue down the field beside the hedge, passing under the widespread branches of a majestic oak. Leave the field by the stile **F**, cross over the road and take the path beside the stream. This is a pleasant, shaded path, but in a dry summer the stream can be little more than a few barely connected puddles. The path emerges into fields, but still continues alongside the stream, which by now has carved itself a deep gully. At a kissing-gate, the path turns away from the stream to head gently uphill to a prominent tree. At the fence turn left and follow it for a short way before turning right through a gate. A large house, Chestal **32**, comes into view, stone-built with tall chimneys, mullioned windows and drip mouldings, which are all the classic marks of an old Cotswold house, but the proportions are wrong. It was in fact built in 1848, and its style is unmistakably Victorian.

Continue in the same direction, following the line of the hedge. Once through the next gate, carry on past a waymark to reach the road. Turn right, then left past an immaculate bowling green with a neat little pavilion. The track ends at The Priory, not an ecclesiastical establishment, but a house built for a local clothier in 1539. Turn left up the road: over to the right is the factory built for Listers, a company that began by making machinery for the local textile industry but became famous for its diesel engines. Another reminder of the industrial past is a house on the left which was once home to Mikail Pedersen, inventor of an extraordinary bicycle. It had a very complex frame and a springy saddle constructed from taut strings. It was said to be the most comfortable bicycle in the world. The road leads up to the centre of Dursley, with its old market house **33**, dating from 1738 and topped by a statue of Queen Anne, looking rather glumly down on the square. Happily, the market is still active and this is still the busy heart of the town.

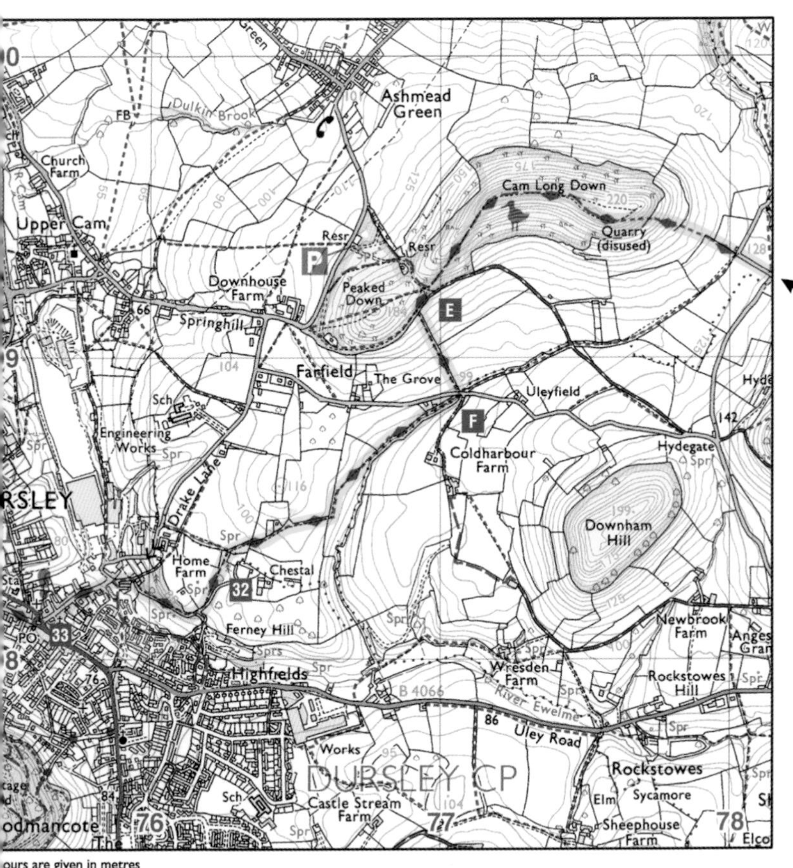

ours are given in metres
vertical interval is 5m

*Stanley woollen mill, famous for its ornate interior of cast-iron colonnades*

## Alternative route from King's Stanley

Cross over the canal and turn left down the towpath. There may be diversions in place during canal restoration, so please follow the official signs. Passing a small pedestrian swing bridge, a rush of water announces the presence of an old mill. This is Ryeford Mill, which has been both a corn mill and a cloth mill, and the sluice gates which admitted water to the wheel can still be seen. This is a quiet, tree-shaded section, with moorhen, mallard and swans sharing the water. The towpath rises beside the double locks, which are joined so that boats can pass straight from one to the other, the central gates being the top gates of the lower chamber and the bottom gates of the higher. The accompanying lock cottage is typical: a simple building, with no decorative features apart from segmented arches over the windows. The bank beside the towpath is full of hedge bindweed, which stays with the path until the next bridge, beyond which is a new housing development. Turn right on to the footpath, opposite the houses **G**, and cross over the mill stream, which served an old oil mill. Cross into the field and turn left to follow the line of the stream.

Where the field narrows, continue on to go through the tunnel under the railway embankment **H**. Turn up the ramp of the cycle track to the left and cross the Ebley bypass at the lights. On the opposite side of the road take the path going up the field past the prominent oak trees. Ignore the obvious track, turning off to the right, and keep going straight up to join the road at Selsley. Turn right and follow the footpath past Stanley Park, an Elizabethan house given the full treatment by the Victorians, who added the exotic details, including an octagonal tower with a spire which now dominates the building. Beyond that is All Saints Church, also Victorian, with its unusual saddleback tower. This is a church with strong associations with the Arts and Crafts movement, with windows by some of the leading exponents, including William Morris, Burne-Jones and Rossetti. Beyond that, at the road junction **I**, cross over to take the footpath that heads half right across the grassland towards the heights of Selsley Common. From the top, there is a commanding view, and although the most prominent buildings in the valley are part of an industrial complex, it is at least one with rural roots – a creamery.

Continue from the top of the hill on the obvious track leading across the plateau towards the buildings beside the road.

The path passes below an old quarry face to reach a gate at the edge of the wood **J**. This leads to a pleasant, woodland path that heads steadily downhill to a broader path. Turn left and continue more or less on the level above the escarpment. The path emerges briefly into the open. Cross straight over the road and take the path, heading back into the wood. Where the paths divide, take the path to the left passing above the house, and now a brisk climb brings a path junction, where the two ways reunite **B.**

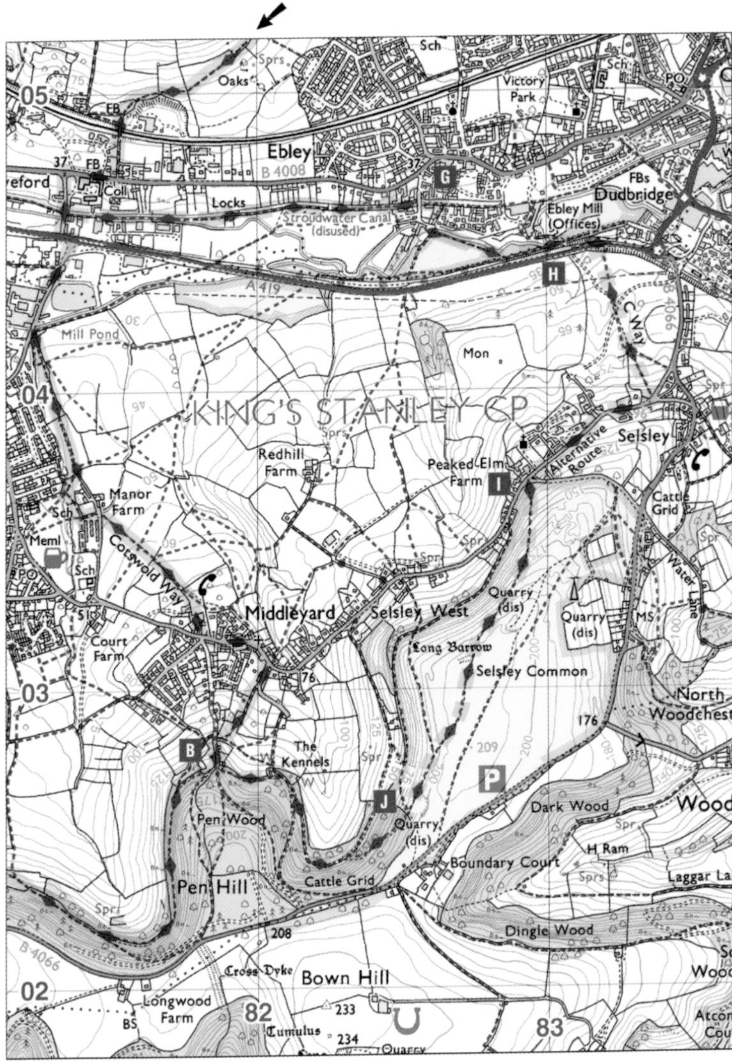


Contours are given in metres
The vertical interval is 5m

*The Stroudwater Navigation is now a quiet backwater, home to a variety of wildfowl, but restoration has begun and this section will soon be busy with boats again.*



# The Stroudwater Navigation

The Stroudwater Navigation, opened in 1779, joined the busy textile centre of Stroud to the River Severn. It was seen primarily as a route to bring cheap coal from Shropshire, the Midlands and the Forest of Dean into the area, and was built to a generous scale, taking vessels up to 70 feet long and 15 feet wide (21.5 by 4.6 metres). This meant that it could be used by the traditional sailing barges of the area, the Severn trows. It became even more important as the 18th century progressed and steam power began to be applied to the woollen industry. Just as modern industry is attracted to sites with motorway access, so the woollen manufacturers turned to the new canal as a centre for development. Two outstanding new mills appeared alongside the waterway. One was Stanley Mill, built of brick and an early example of a fireproof mill, with brick

arches on iron beams supporting stone floors. Previously textile mills were built with wooden pillars and beams and the combination of highly inflammable material, grease and hot machines often proved disastrous. Stanley Mill has a magnificent interior, but the other mill, nearby Ebley, is notable for its elegant exterior, having something of the style of a French château. Stanley is still in business, but Ebley has been taken over and refurbished as the local council offices.

Decline in both the woollen industry and canal traffic led to closure in 1954, but in recent years canals have enjoyed a revival, carrying tourists instead of coal. The long process of reconstruction is now under way, and there are long-term hopes that the work will continue eastwards to the Thames and Severn Canal, which the Stroudwater joins. If that is achieved, then Britain's two great rivers, the Thames and the Severn, will be reunited.

# 11 Dursley to Wotton-under-Edge

*7.3 miles (11.8 km); short route 4.8 miles (7.8 km)*
*Parking: Swimming Pool, grid reference ST 755983, long stay, no charge*

**Ascent** 835 feet (260 metres)
**Descent** 836 feet (255 metres)
**Lowest point** Dursley 246 feet (75 metres)
**Highest point** Stinchcombe Hill 689 feet (210 metres)

Leave the main square by the pedestrian street to the right and at the end turn left, then right past the bus station and The Old Spot pub. Take the road that leads steeply uphill and where that turns sharply to the left **A** turn right up the track into the wood. Paths immediately divide and the route goes to the left, continuing uphill. This is a good, broad path that provides a long but steady climb through this attractive area, where the trees seem to have a precarious hold on the steep slope. Everything is very peaceful, apart from the somewhat repetitive coo-cooing of wood pigeons. At the top of the hill, continue straight on beside the fence to emerge by the golf clubhouse on the edge of the plateau of Stinchcombe Hill **B**. There is now a choice of routes: the direct and the scenic. The direct alternative is short and simple: head straight off across the golf course, on the route marked by wooden posts, to head for the obvious gap in the woodland opposite **C**. The longer offical route is highly recommended for those who enjoy a comfortable walk around the edge with fine views all the way. The long route is also basically very simple. Turn right at the clubhouse, continue across the grass to the edge of the wood and follow it round, all the time staying close to the escarpment edge. The path now stays with the edge in a convoluted route until it eventually arrives, after briefly dipping down into scrub, at a sharp promontory, Drakestone Point **34**. Here is the best of the view, which stretches down the Severn from the cranes and warehouses of Sharpness to the two modern road bridges near Bristol. There is a topograph and a shelter with an attractive weather vane showing a plus-foured golfer trying to hit his way out of a bunker. The path now doubles back along the opposite side of the promontory to continue alongside the wood, until the gap **C** is reached.

Enter the woodland to take the stony path heading downhill round to the left. As the trees clear, those who have taken the short route have a consolation view of the Severn bridges. At the foot of the hill turn left over the footbridge; turn left again at the gate to take the path with the fence on the right. The path runs above the formal parkland of the handsome house,

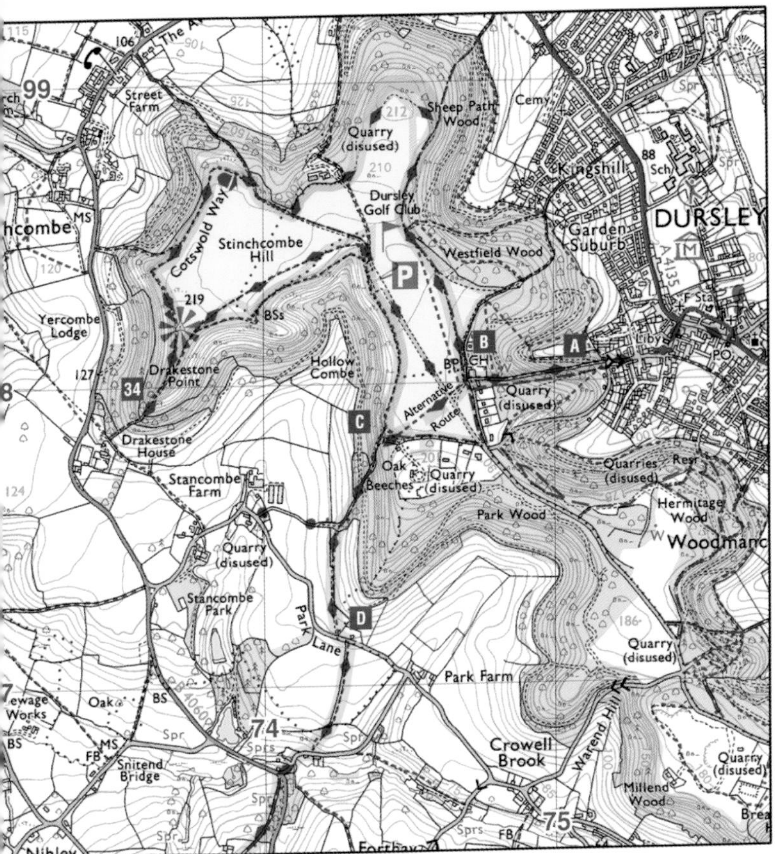

ours are given in metres
vertical interval is 5m

Stancombe Park, heading towards the village of North Nibley and the monument on the hill. The path traverses the hill and continues to a kissing-gate at the far side of the field. Continue down to the next gate **D** and turn left on to the road. After about 30 paces turn right at the next gate and head straight across the middle of the field. Do not be deterred by the fact that the field may be planted with crops, even if, as it was when the author came this way, the crops consist of maize rising above head height. Leaving this field brings more comfortable grassland. Go through the gate and across the field to a waymark by the telegraph poles. Bear right at the post to the gate by the house and continue to the road, then turn right where, in a kind gesture, a supply of chilled water has been supplied for walkers. Cross over the stream with an attractive pond alongside. Cross straight over the B-road and once again take a path leading into a wood.

*These striking conifers above Wotton-under-Edge are replacements for trees originally planted in 1815 to celebrate the victory of Waterloo.*



This broad track runs close to the edge of the woodland and is worn down to the bedrock. Where the woodland ends, the path is closed in by hedgerows, which provide an accompaniment down to North Nibley. Another rather grand house appears, 17th-century Nibley House **35**, and the path runs directly into Lowerhouse Lane. At the end turn left at the main road through the village, known simply as The Street. A large stone house has been gentrified by the addition of a brick façade, with ornamental windows and an imposing door with pediment and fanlight. A far more modest row of cottages must once have been made up of very tiny houses, but several have been knocked together, as can be seen from the filled-in front doors. Turn right at the main road, and after a short way cross over to take the broad track heading uphill through the trees. This is a deep sunken lane, but it is soon abandoned for a flight of steps on the right heading up to the monument. The climb is very steep, but a handrail offers welcome assistance all the way to the top. Eventually it emerges right at the monument **36**. Built in 1866, it stands over 100 feet (33 metres) high and has an internal staircase leading up to a viewing gallery. Anyone prepared to climb the hill twice can get the key from the village shop. The carved legend tells the story of William Tyndale. He was born in North Nibley in 1484 and took advantage of the new printing presses to provide the first complete translation of the Bible into English. He was accused of heresy and burned at the stake in France in 1536.

After the climb, it comes as a special pleasure to find that the next section of the walk is over level grassland along the escarpment, once again passing a topograph detailing the different points of interest, which includes a distant view of the next tall monument that will be met along the way. The walk stays beside the fence at the edge before plunging once more into the trees. At the first track division continue straight on, but at the next take the track turning off to the right **E**. The path enters an area of mixed woodland, which brings the sweet smell of pine. Unlike so many woodland walks along the way, it remains very much on the level. It skirts the earthworks of Brackenbury Ditches, the ramparts of an Iron Age hill fort **37**.

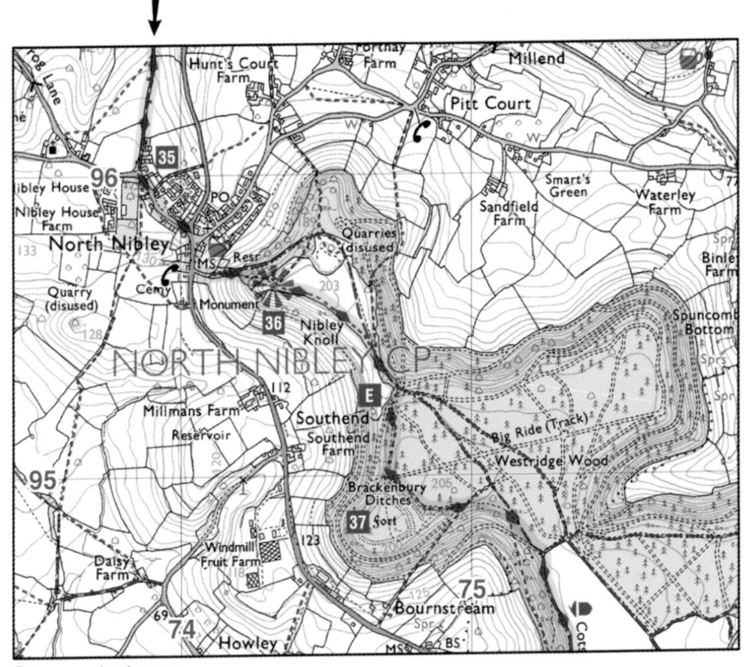

Contours are given in metres
The vertical interval is 5m

At the edge of the wood turn right to continue in the same general direction, with the field on your left. At the end of the field, where the track begins to swing left, look out for a gate on the right almost hidden in the hedge. The path now emerges into the open by a curious stand of conifers surrounded by a circular stone wall **38**. The trees were first planted in 1815 to commemorate the battle of Waterloo, and have twice been renewed. The path heads to the left of this enclosure, heading downhill to a marker post, where a narrow footpath is joined which continues on down to the road at Wotton-under-Edge.

Continue walking on towards the town, and at the sign for the town centre turn right past an interestingly varied terrace of houses, heading for the High Street with its ornate clock, celebrating Victoria's Jubilee. This is yet another wool town, boasting a number of fine clothiers' houses, many displaying

***The path leading out of Wotton-under-Edge.***

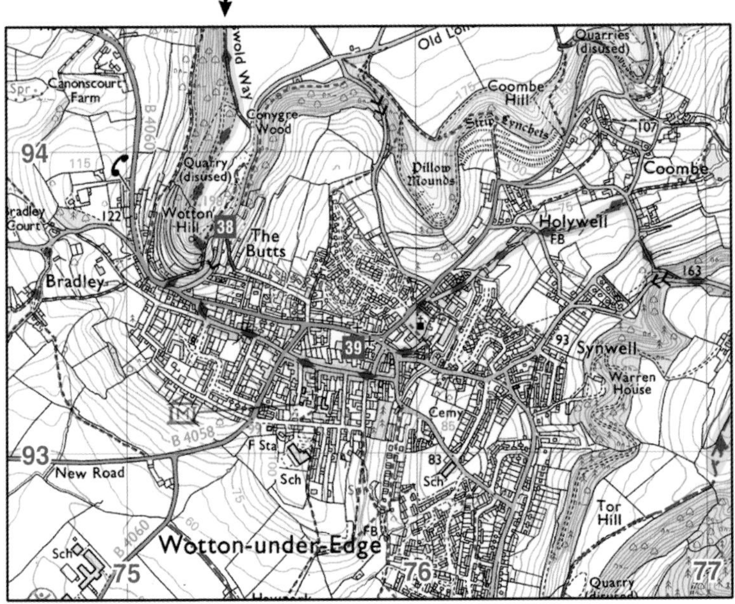

Contours are given in metres
The vertical interval is 5m

grand features – a notable example is the ornate doorway to what is now a bank. Turn left down Church Street, where it is well worth pausing for a moment to visit Hugh Perry's almshouses **39**. Hugh Perry was born in the town, but went on to become Sheriff of London in 1632. He bequeathed the money to build the almshouses for six poor men and six poor women, with strict conditions about religious observance. You can walk into the courtyard to find an enchanting group of buildings, particularly notable for their complex stone roofs, curving round dormer windows. The tiny chapel is still regularly used and is illuminated by a stained-glass window showing sheep and wool spinners.

At the end of the street cross the road and take the high-level footpath that curves away from the road. Go down Shinbone Alley, a curious name with no obvious origin, and turn left into the churchyard. This is yet another splendid Cotswold church, dating back to the 14th century but, like many others, radically altered by the Victorians. It is still well worth taking a look inside at some of the remaining features. There is a resplendent organ donated by George I in 1726 with an array of gilded pipes, which must have a tremendous effect in this immense space. The main interest, however, lies with the monuments, which range from a brass showing Thomas, Lord Berkeley and his wife to neoclassical carvings of the 18th century. Continuing through the churchyard, turn right at the road. Opposite is another row of almshouses, almost submerged by new development. After a short way, turn right on to the lane that goes left to head out of town.

*The tower of the Tyndale Monument, built to commemorate William Tyndale, translater of The Bible into English.*

# 12 Wotton-under-Edge to Hawkesbury

*7.4 miles (11.9 km)*
*Parking: Potters Pond, grid reference ST 759933, long stay, no charge*

**Ascent** 984 feet (300 metres)
**Descent** 623 feet (190 metres)
**Lowest point** Lower Kilcott 246 feet (75 metres)
**Highest point** Black Quarries Hill 705 feet (215 metres)

The path out of town runs alongside a busy little stream, brightened in summer with golden saxifrage, yellow flag and other typical water plants. There is a right and left dog-leg at the hamlet of Holywell **A**, after which the path continues to follow the stream. Over to the left is Coombe Hill with a very prominent set of strip lynchets **40**. These are cultivation terraces created by medieval farmers to enable them to plough their strips on the steep side of the hill. At the road, turn right and just before reaching the crest of the hill, turn left up the private road by the houses, then almost immediately right up the steps to a sunken lane, overhung by trees. A steep climb leads up to a road, with an exaggerated zig-zag near the top to ease the slope. Turn left again on to the road, still going uphill, but rather more gently, through farmland. The road passes Warren Farm, which announces possession of a pedigree herd of French cattle, though the only cows in sight were very definitely home grown. Woodland now comes in on the left; shortly after that **B** turn sharply to the right by the entrance to Newark Park. The path passes a hump in the field on the left, which is Blackquarries Hill long barrow. This is a fine, airy, high-level walk with outstanding views, and the area is also home to partridge, which can occasionally be spotted, waddling along like plump businessmen. The path once again arrives at the escarpment with views to the west, out towards the Mendips and more distant Quantock hills.

Where the farm track turns to the left, carry straight on up the ridge to the edge of the woodland, and then turn sharp left to take the path at the edge of the wood. Where the path divides, carry straight on into an area of conifers. At a large clearing, carry straight on along the narrow path to the right, a stony way which passes through tangled, overgrown woodland. Where the path divides **C**, continue down a very deep sunken lane, heading downhill. In spring, the path is bright with wood violets and primroses, but in summer the most prominent plants are the glossy hart's-tongue ferns. As the path descends, the banks get higher and higher and the path ever gloomier, with erosion exposing the gnarled tree roots. At the foot of this long descent, the path emerges into the open to farmland again. Carry straight on down to the road, cross straight over to a gate **D** and head across the field on a diagonal, aiming for a marker post by the telegraph poles. There is a gate in the far corner of the field, which leads to a second gate and a bridge across the stream. Cross over and turn right to follow the stream that trickles down over rock to provide an accompaniment to the tree-shaded walk. Over to the left is a small reservoir and pumping station, and this water supply once served a small mill, which, like most in the area, was at various times used both for grinding grain and for fulling cloth. The name, Monk's Mill, suggests considerable antiquity, and records date back over 500 years. Carry on to the the broad track leading up to the road **E**.

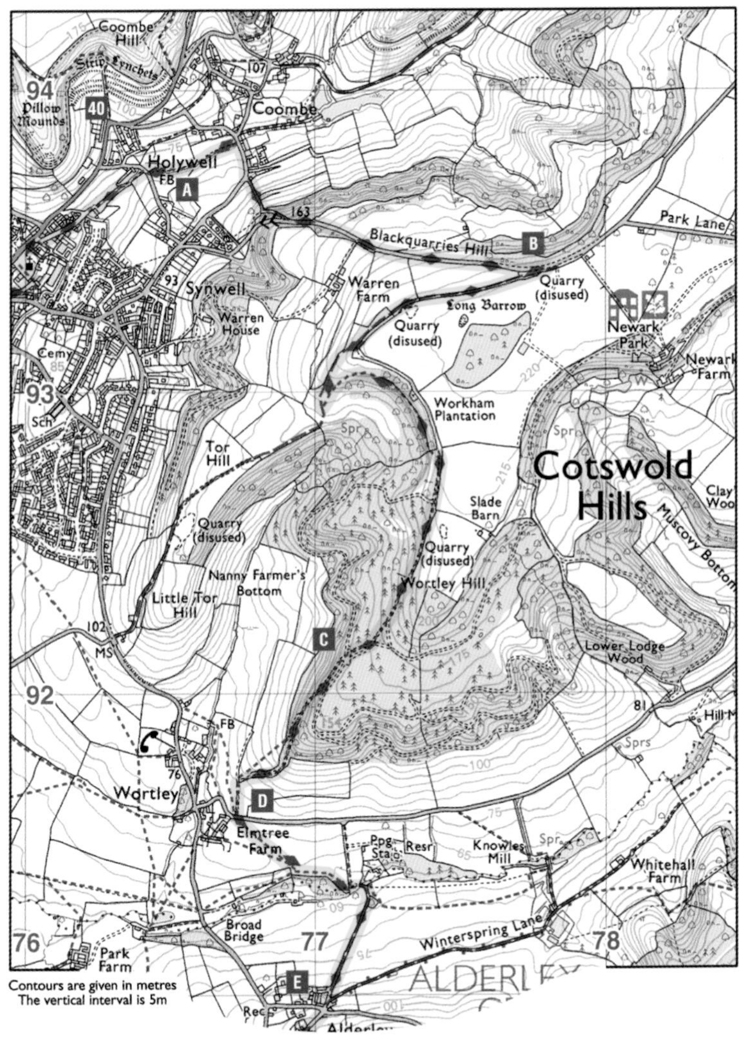

Contours are given in metres
The vertical interval is 5m

At the road, turn right into the hamlet of Alderley, which is distinguished by some very fine Cotswold vernacular architecture: a row of cottages with stone slate roofs and dormer windows. The route goes past a grand gateway, with a mounting block alongside, and heads for the centre of the village. The church that comes into view has a curious quirk: presumably unable to afford a vaulted ceiling, an elaborate fan vault has been painted on to create a *trompe-l'œil* effect. The Elizabethan mansion, now a school, seems almost overwhelmed by its massive chimneys, while the elegant 18th-century house tucks everything away behind a parapet. Turn left at the T-junction, then continue straight down the track that runs along the lower slopes of a grassy hill crowned by trees. This enters a beautiful, peaceful valley with strip lynchets on either side as evidence of medieval farming. But over to the right is Hillesley Mill and a little further along, past a short section where the path dives into woodland, is Newmills Farm **41** down in the bottom of the valley. The latter actually was a new mill in the 17th century and in 1806 some of the first power looms in the area were installed there: this quiet spot once rivalled the textile towns of Yorkshire and Lancashire as a centre of innovation. Further memories of those days survive in field names, such as Rack Close, an area where cloth was once set out to dry. It is now difficult to imagine such a scene. At the end of the path, turn right on to a broad track, then left on to a quiet country lane leading into Lower Kilcott.

## Kilcott Mill

**Kilcott Mill, close to the turning down to Hillesley, was a grain mill not a textile mill, and is one of the very few in the area still to have working machinery. A mill was first recorded on this site in Domesday Book, but was completely rebuilt in 1655 and powered by water from the pond supplied by the Kilcott brook. The mill house was added in 1677.**

The road arrives at the main group of houses, backed by a stand of immense larch trees **F**. Turn right on to the track up the hill. Where tracks divide, continue uphill on the track to the left, cross a stile and take the path round to the right. The path follows the line of a high hedge into an area of woodland. Where a wide track appears on the left **G**, turn left to follow the edge of the wood. Where the woodland ends, turn right to take the wide path that heads up towards the Somerset monument **42**. This curiously oriental-looking monument has nothing to do with the Far East nor, geographically, with Somerset. It was built to commemorate the achievements of General Lord Robert Somerset, whose main claim to fame was his role in the Battle of Waterloo.

Turn left on to the road heading down to Hawkesbury Upton, which announces its presence with a rather ominous sign, saying 'You'll never leave.' The road arrives at the old drovers' pond, where generations of drovers stopped to water their cattle. Today, there is little trace of water and only the bullrushes give any real indication that it was ever a pond at all.

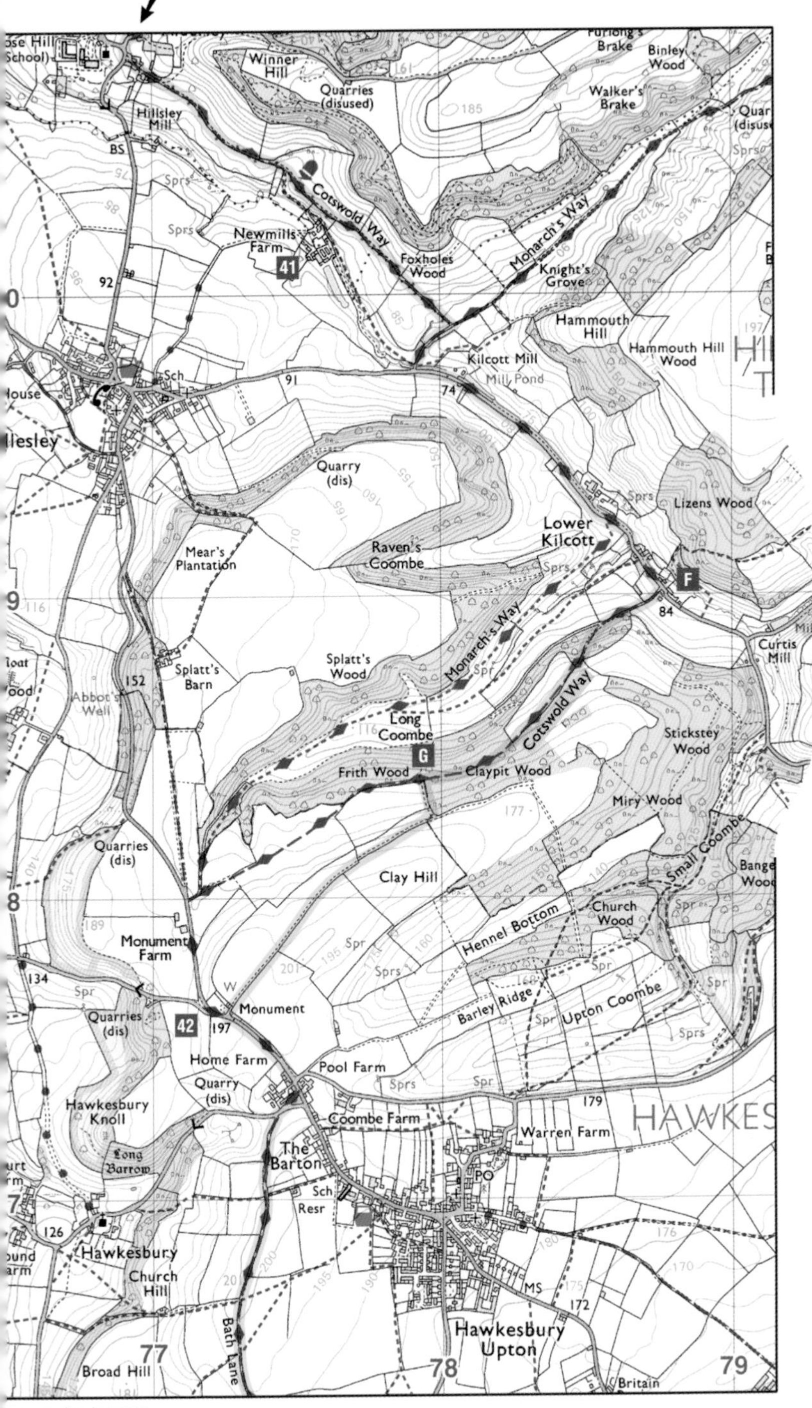


…ours are given in metres
…e vertical interval is 5m

# 13 Hawkesbury to Tormarton

*7.7 miles (12.4 km)*
*Parking: Parking: no designated parking – please park considerately*

**Ascent** 476 feet (145 metres)
**Descent** 590 feet (180 metres)
**Lowest point** Little Sodbury 410 feet (125 metres)
**Highest point** Hawkesbury 656 feet (200 metres)

Once past the pond, turn left on to the broad track, with views out across the Severn Vale once more, but now the river itself is out of sight, screened by the nearby hills. The track heads down towards a quiet road, but just before reaching it **A** turn off to take the path beside the hedge. Stay alongside the road as far as a gate near a ruined barn, then head across the field on a diagonal. This ends as a confusion of tracks, most of which form part of a motocross track, but the walk continues along the narrow path beside the hedge. This dips briefly into woodland with some fine, mature trees, of which the grandest appear as a line of beech accompanying the path.

***The track leading off to the distant ramparts of Sodbury Camp.***

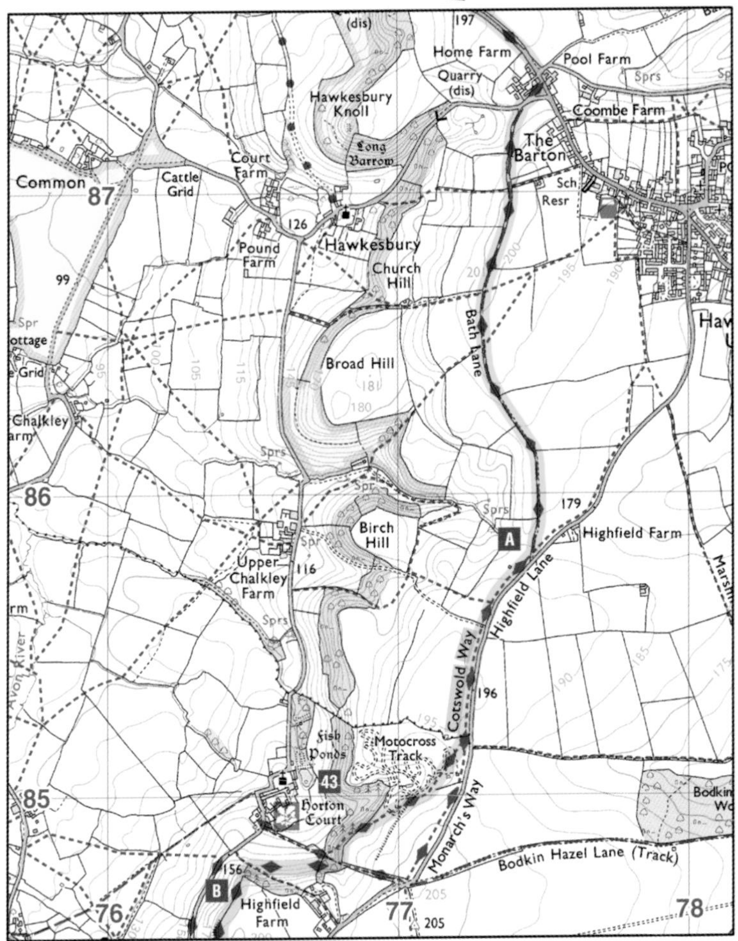


Contours are given in metres
The vertical interval is 5m

On leaving the wood, the path traverses the face of the hill, this time offering views out across the length of the Cotswold escarpment, back to the now distant Tyndale monument. Horton Court **43** comes into view down in the valley – a house of great antiquity, the oldest part of which dates back to the 12th century. It sits comfortably snuggled down into a hollow, shielded by trees, including a number of large copper beech, and is approached by a processional row of holm oak. The old hall house has been much extended over the centuries, additions including a typical Cotswold manor and a charming, if slightly incongruous, Italianate loggia. It is now in the care of the National Trust. The route heads towards the right-hand fringe of the woodland **B**. **T**urn left through the gate and take the path that zig-zags up through the wood. At the top of the hill, go through the gate and follow the path round the edge of the field to arrive at a

Old Sodbury church.

small triangular hill fort. Follow the path across the fort on a diagonal to the left-hand corner, emerging above the parkland of a very fine early 19th-century house. The architects have made the most of the spectacular situation by providing bay windows reaching the full height of the façade. Go through the gate at the edge of the grounds and head towards the little tower. This is not, as it seems at first sight, either a folly or a dovecote, but a modern structure, built to provide nesting space for swallows and barn owls. Few birds enjoy such elegant residences. From here, the path goes steadily downhill. Ignore the path down through the woods and continue straight on to the village of Horton, emerging by the old village school. Turn left then right at the road junction and after a short distance left on to the path just beyond the old Post Office **C**.

The path begins by running between high hedges, but soon emerges to continue in the same direction straight across the field. At the end of the field, it dips steeply down to a hollow and then climbs back up again to arrive at a small reservoir, which has now become an attractive feature, fringed by reed beds. The route continues straight on via stiles and gates to a stile beside a house at the edge of Little Sodbury. Turn left, then right at the road, and at the next junction turn left past the church. This was built in the 19th century, using stone from the old chapel of the manor house. The church itself has a special place in English religious history, for it was the preaching that he heard here that inspired William Tyndale to take on the great task of translating the Bible. The quiet road continues through this very pleasant hamlet, where one resident keeps bees and pots of honey are on sale in season from a wayside stand. The circular humps in the surrounding fields are reminders of a now almost forgotten form of animal husbandry. These are pillow mounds, constructed for rabbit warrens. The rabbits must have thought how kind it was to provide such excellent homes, unaware of their ultimate destination, not in a comfortable burrow but in the pot. The road leads up past a series of ponds on the left; at the top of the rise, follow the road round to the left, then turn immediately left up the path **D**. Where the way divides, carry straight on along the broad track heading steadily uphill. Near the brow of the hill bear right, still going uphill to reach a kissing-gate. This emerges by the ditch and ramparts of Sodbury Camp, probably the finest and best-preserved Iron Age hill fort to be met along the Way **44**. It has widely spaced double ramparts and encloses an area of over 10 acres (4 hectares). The path goes straight through the middle of the fort and offers views all across the surrounding countryside: whoever lived here, they were not going to be surprised by unwelcome visitors.

Leaving the fort, carry straight on towards a gate beside the trees. Turn right to take the path heading downhill through woodland, and where the path levels out turn left towards the gate **E**.

Now a grand view opens out in front. Once through the gate, turn sharp left to follow the path beside the field, heading towards the village. On reaching a tall sycamore, take the obvious path going round the hill and heading down to Old Sodbury. The path ends at the road, close to the local school, which has a very charming pair of gates, showing a boy and a girl reading books. The route now goes through the churchyard. The church itself **45** is well worth a visit, for although it has been heavily restored it

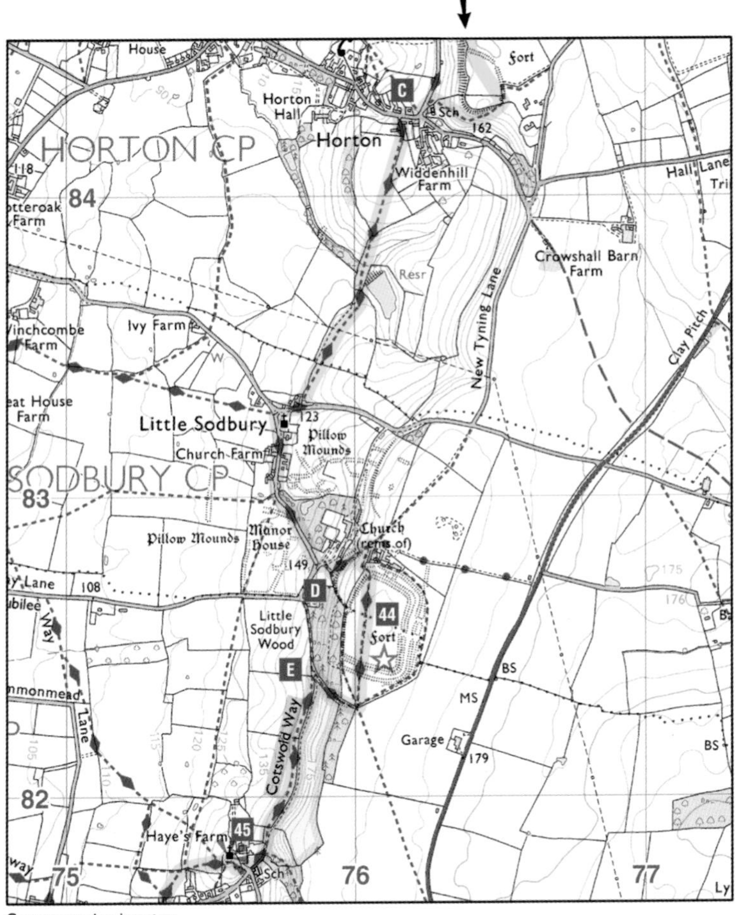

Contours are given in metres
The vertical interval is 5m

has a couple of interesting and unusual features. In an ornate recess in the north transept is a pair of 13th-century effigies: one is conventionally carved from stone and shows a peculiarly pigeon-toed knight reclining under a shield, but the other is a rare example carved in wood, one of the few survivors of an old Bristol-based craft. The other oddity is in the chancel, a century-old bier, once used for wheeling coffins into the church.

Carry on through the churchyard to reach the edge of the hill, where a

*This charming ornamental bridge was designed to fit the elegance of the parkland of Dodington House.*

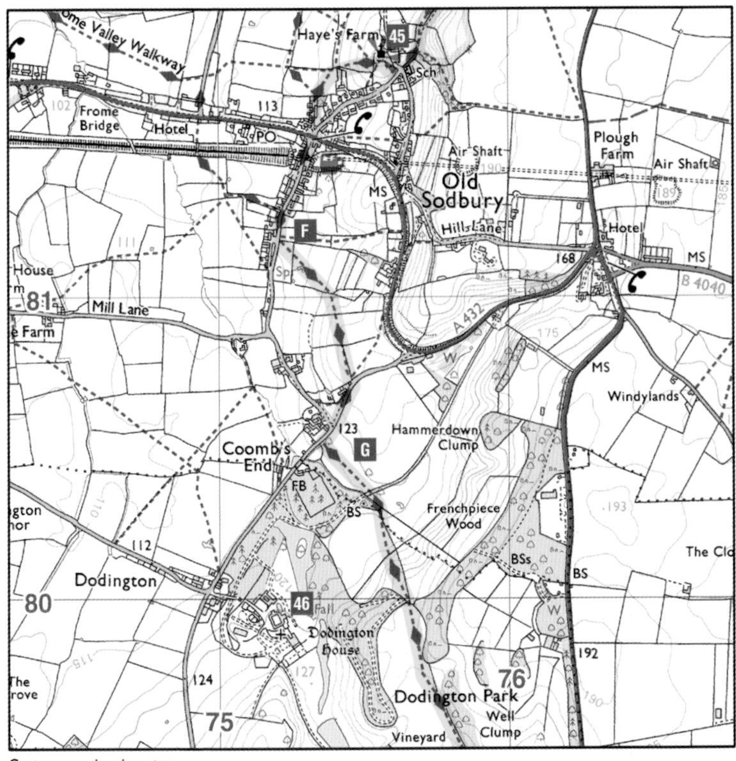

Contours are given in metres
The vertical interval is 5m

topograph identifies the distant hills as the Brecon Beacons. The path leads straight down the hill to the corner of the field, then across the next field to the buildings and the busy main road. Cross straight over by the inn and go down Chapel Lane. The chapel itself, built in 1835, has now been converted into a house. Just past the school sign **F**, turn left through the gate and head diagonally across the field, aiming to the right of a clump of trees. The path goes steadily uphill through a series of gates and, although it never reaches the heights of the earlier part of the walk, it still gives excellent views over the valley with its neatly squared-off fields. Join the road by the house and turn right. As a reminder that this really still is the Cotswolds, there is an old house with prominent gables, absolutely typical of the region. Carry straight on at the road junction, and then turn left opposite Dennison Cottage **G** to return to the fields. The route goes straight across the field and crosses over the driveway to Dodington House. The whole area has the typical appearance of parkland, with trees carefully placed to create picturesque effects. At the gate, cross the stream on an ornamental bridge, then turn left to follow the line of the fence heading steadily uphill. Dodington House itself **46** comes into view on the right and a wide vista opens up. Head for the gap between two patches of woodland and once the top of the hill is reached turn slightly left towards a

*Tormarton was originally 'Tower Marton' and takes its name from the massive Norman tower of the church.*

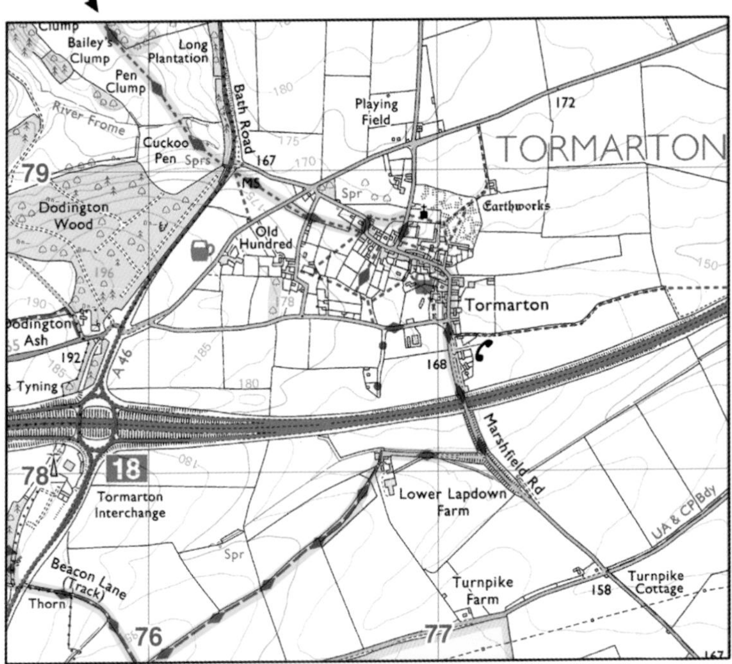


Contours are given in metres
The vertical interval is 5m

marker post by the wood. The path follows the edge of the woodland above a delightful little valley, closed in by trees on all sides. This is still parkland, and the walk runs past a majestic solitary oak to a stand of horse chestnut. Here the path turns diagonally left towards the head of the valley and comes down to a footbridge over the stream. Turn left, gradually moving away uphill from the line of the stream This is all pleasant, easy walking on grass cropped short by sheep and ends at a gate at the end of the line of taller trees. It then comes as something of a shock to find this lovely rural walk exchanged for a busy main road.

**Tormarton Church**

**Many interesting features can be seen in Tormarton Church. The first two stages of the tower and the chancel arch are Norman; the font is 13th century and the pulpit Jacobean. There are a number of fine brasses and monuments.**

Cross straight over the road and take the field path opposite. The road has obviously been realigned at some time, because an old milestone now stands forlorn and unnoticed, all but lost in the undergrowth. Carry straight on across the B-road and a minor road towards Tormarton. On reaching the houses, turn left and, after a short way, turn right over a stile and head towards the church.

Turn right at the stile opposite the church and continue on down to the road, turning left by The Portcullis inn and a large pond, then follow Marshfield Road round to the right to leave the village.

# 14 Tormarton to Cold Ashton

*6.6 miles (10.6 km)*
*Parking: Picnic Area M4/A46 interchange, grid reference ST 756777, toilets, no charge*

**Ascent** 558 feet (170 metres)
**Descent** 410 feet (125 metres)
**Lowest point** Dyrham 377 feet (115 metres)
**Highest point** Cold Ashton 672 feet (205 metres)

The road out of Tormarton leads past a pair of very attractive cottages and then heads off for the bridge over the M4. Once across, take the first turning on the right **A**. Follow this minor road to the end, then turn left at the large shed. Continue between the two houses on to the green track. This is a very different landscape from anything met so far. The grey, stony Cotswold

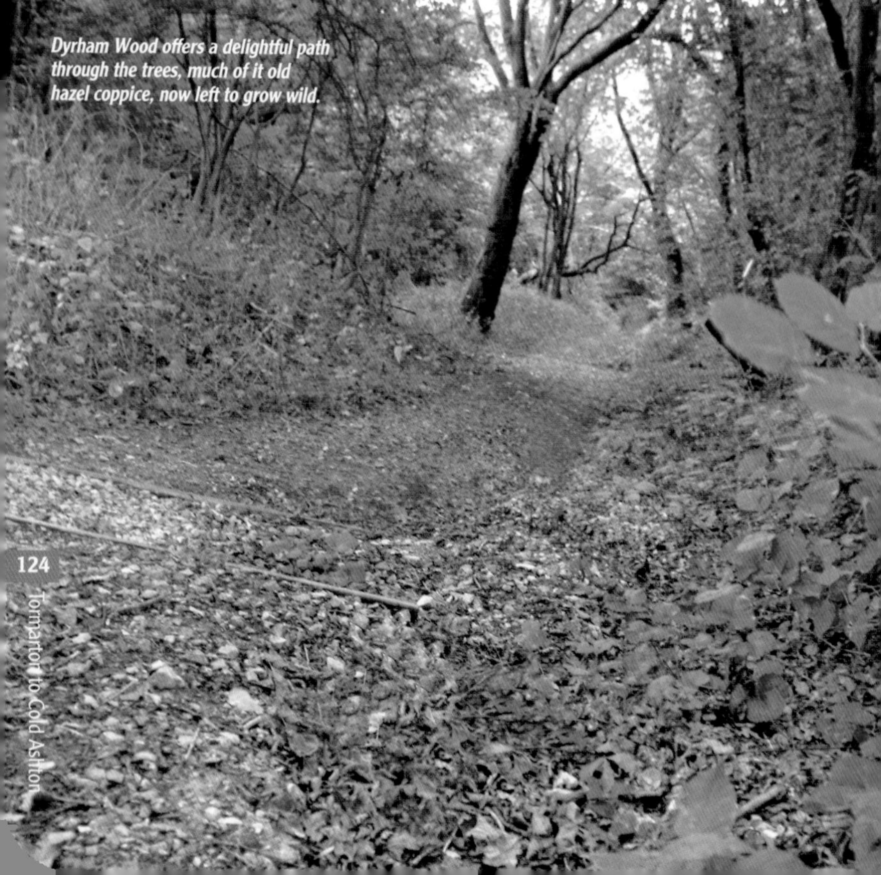

*Dyrham Wood offers a delightful path through the trees, much of it old hazel coppice, now left to grow wild.*

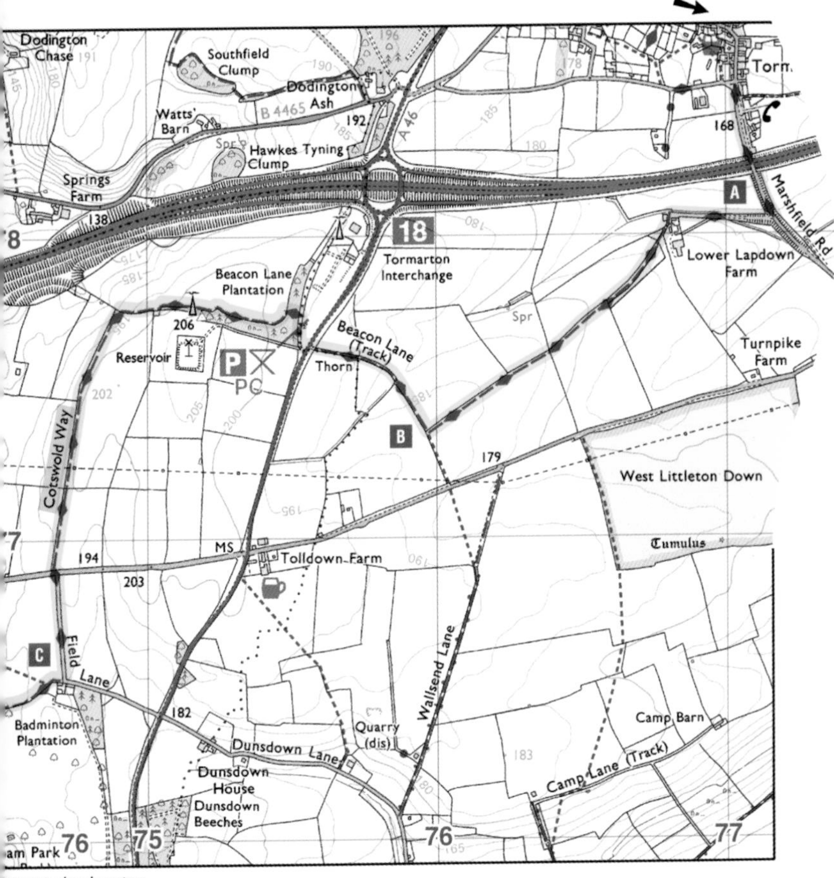


ours are given in metres
vertical interval is 5m

soil has given way to a rich, red soil, and the grazing fields have been replaced by the enormous open arable fields of modern farming. At a track junction **B** turn right, heading back towards the main road down the green lane bordered by hedges. Turn left at the road to cross via the traffic island, then turn back to the right by the trees to the parking and picnic area and then turn left into the wood. Emerging from the trees, turn left to follow the edge of the woodland. The landscape is still one of enormous fields, but the path is heading back to the escarpment, though considerably lower than when it was last encountered. It does, however, herald the arrival of much more attractive scenery. The path heads off towards a little scooped-out valley, but before reaching it, swings off to the left. After this diversion to the east to get across the motorway, the Way returns to its southerly course. The path runs beside a hedge of mainly hawthorn and elder, down to a minor road. Continue in the same direction on the road opposite, and on reaching the barns **C** turn right on to the path beside the high stone wall.

# Dyrham Park

The house was built for William Blathwayt, on the site of a Tudor manor that had been inherited by his wife. Blathwayt became Secretary of State under William III in 1692, a position which provided more than adequate funds for this grand house, which presents two different faces to the world. The west front was designed by a relatively unknown French architect and has a distinctly Parisian air; the architect of the east front was William Talman, Wren's right-hand man, and is gloriously baroque. The gardens were originally in the formal Dutch style – and the interior also has Dutch themes. But by the late 18th-century the Dutch water gardens had gone, to be replaced by a typical English parkland, now famous for its herds of deer. The Cotswold Way skirts the park, but the house is revealed in its full glory when the walk comes into Dyrham village.

*The statue of Neptune in Dyrham Park.*

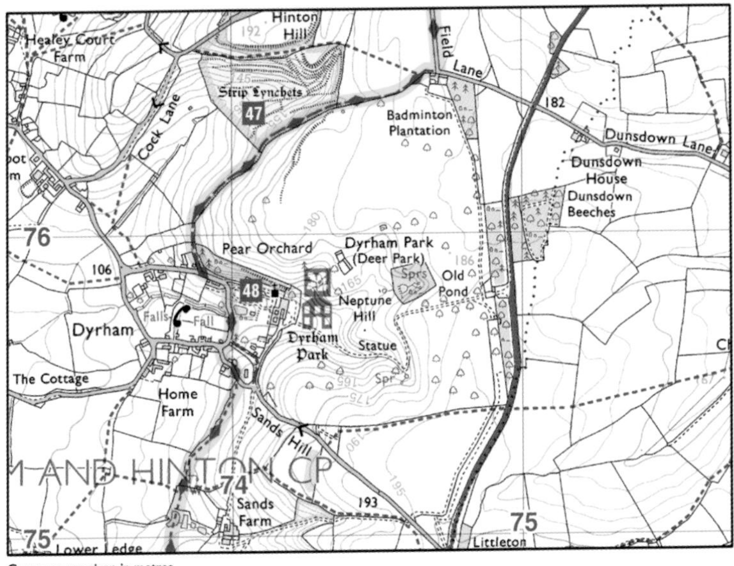


Contours are given in metres
The vertical interval is 5m

The route now runs round the edge of Dyrham Park, famous for its deer, which remain frustratingly out of sight behind the wall. The wall itself, however, is a magnificent example of drystone walling at its very best. The path now runs along the rim of a lovely deep valley **47** which boasts tiers of strip lynchets. One cannot help contrasting these terraces, hacked with great effort into the hillside, with the large ploughed fields so very close by. Looking out on to the plain brings another old pattern of fields, all quite small and in a bewildering variety of strange shapes. This is a splendid section of the Way, combining good surfaces underfoot with a varied and beautiful landscape. It comes as a disappointment when it all ends at a gate and a path leading down into Dyrham – but there are other delights in store in compensation.

The houses are full of character, though one hides away behind an elaborate gateway topped by a coat of arms. An old stone house with mullioned windows is followed by one in which the front door is not only very low but actually sunk down below road level. Then comes the entrance to Dyrham Park **48** itself, a house unmistakably designed to impress. Continue on to the road junction and turn left. Just before the road begins to swing to the left, turn off to take the footpath on the right.

It may be exciting to have a glimpse of wealth and splendour, but it is no less pleasant to return to field paths and country views. The path runs along by the hedge at the foot of a gentle slope and then continues along a little path, tightly closed in by hedges. This ends at an ornamental hedge with a large weeping willow trailing its branches over the water. Carry straight on across

*Cold Ashton is notable for its grand buildings: even the entrance to the manor is monumentally imposing.*



the middle of the next field, heading off towards the patch of woodland. Look for the gap in the trees to find a footbridge, and once across head on a diagonal towards the wood on the left. Follow the edge of the wood, and then take the path through the trees. This is an area of old hazel coppice, but has now become an unruly jumble. There is a steady climb, which passes the Dyrham Wood message box, where visitors can pick up any news or make a note of anything they have spotted that might interest others who come this way.

The path emerges into the open again and is bordered by buddleia, shrubs that are particularly attractive to butterflies, and on a fine summer day you can expect to see several different species. The path runs down to the road; cross straight over to the next field path and turn left beside the hedge. At the next gap go through the hedge and turn right on a path that leads to a little lane running down to the main road. Cross straight over and take the path that heads on a diagonal across the field to the far corner, then continue on a diagonal across the next field to yet another busy A-road. Turn left towards The White Hart and cross the road to take the grassy path between the drive and the stone wall. This leads on to the churchyard at Cold Ashton **49**. It is an unassuming building with a squat tower, but has one grand and elaborate feature: a canopied pulpit of the early 16th century. From the churchyard go down to the road and turn right on to the main road through the village.

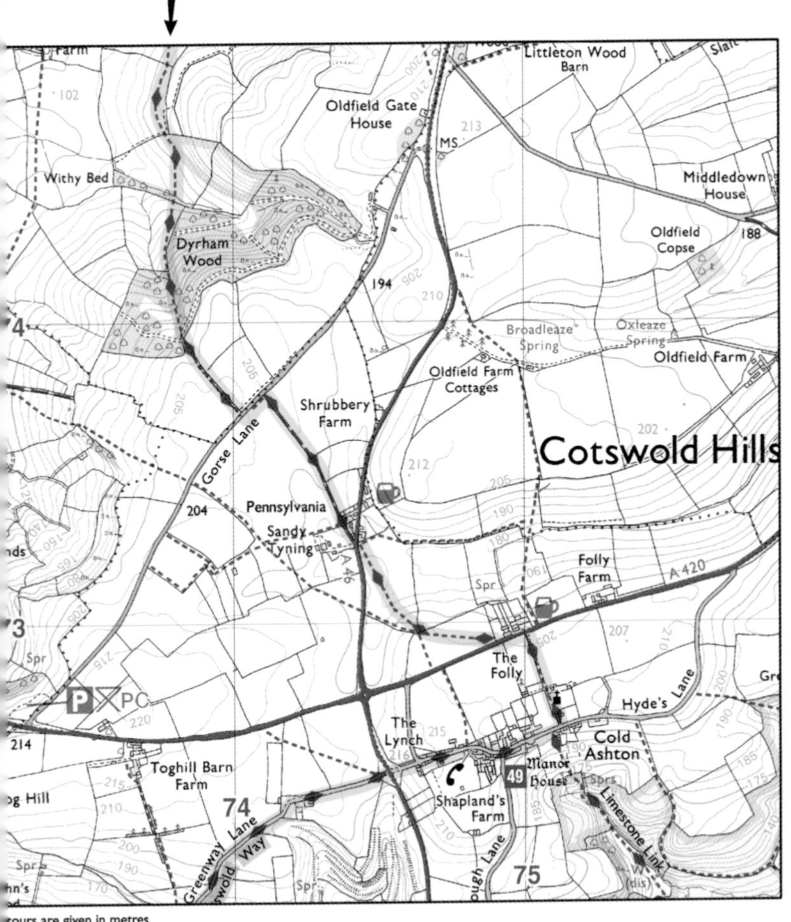


tours are given in metres
e vertical interval is 5m

# 15 Cold Ashton to Bath

*10.2 miles (16.5 km)*
*Parking: parish hall, grid reference ST 747725, voluntary payment. For parking in Bath consult Bath Tourist Information Centre*

**Ascent** 738 feet (225 metres)
**Descent** 1,312 feet (400 metres)
**Lowest point** Bath Abbey 82 feet (25 metres)
**Highest point** Prospect Stile 754 feet (230 metres)

Cold Ashton was originally part of the Bath Abbey estate, but its commanding position at the rim of the hill made it very attractive to the wealthy landowners who came later. Continue on past the fine Elizabethan manor, which has an almost equally grand rectory as its next door neighbour. Ignore the turning to the left, and where the road divides **A** take the turn to the left, going downhill towards the main road. Cross straight over and continue on the mercifully peaceful country lane on the far side. This is another attractive and interesting section, with an undulating landscape of green fields and more unmistakable strip lynchets on the hillside. Reaching a group of barns, keep following the road round to the left; the views are temporarily lost behind high hedges. The road soon re-emerges into the open to more fine views of grassy hills and a house and farm on the hill to the right, which enjoy

***Ford Hall Lane on the approach to Lansdown.***

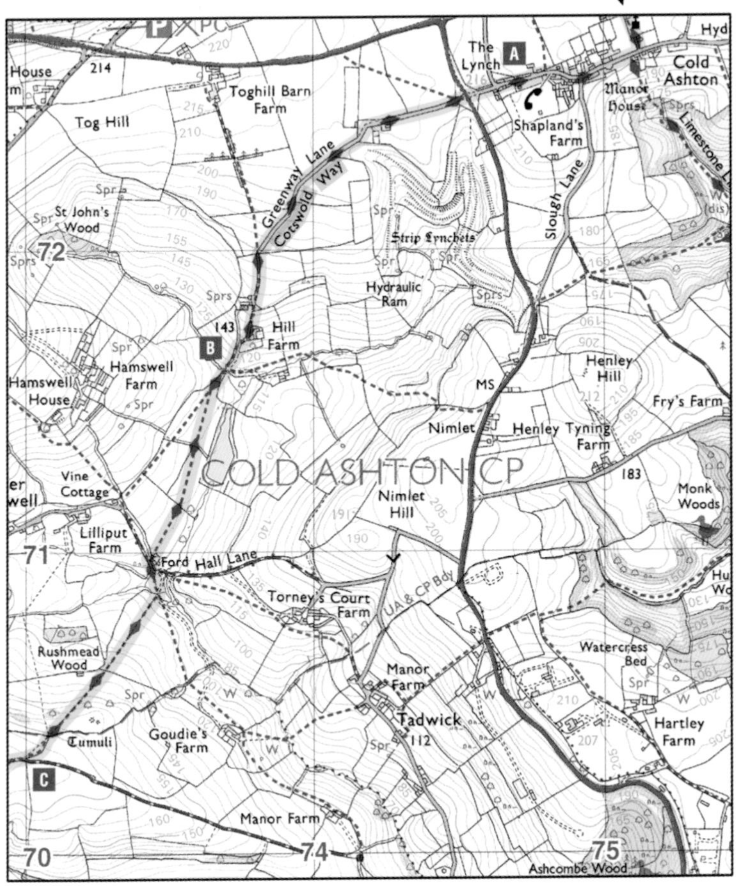


Contours are given in metres
The vertical interval is 5m

a most enviable situation. The road runs between verges which in summer are rich with wild flowers of as many as a dozen different species, ranging from the delicate white of stitchwort to the rich purple of scabious. Continue past a plant nursery, and now the road begins to go steeply downhill, going straight on down a farm approach road and passing some magnificent old oaks. Where the road turns sharply to the left **B**, continue straight on to take the path through a patch of woodland. Carry on in the same direction across the fields, eventually heading to the right of the farm.

Reaching the road, turn left, cross over a pair of cattle grids, and then turn half-right to head up the hill. The path passes through an obvious gap in the trees to reach the rim of the hill, where someone has kindly supplied a bench for walkers to admire the view or simply recover their breath. From here, turn half-right towards a gate in the gap in the hedge, then cross the next field to the green lane **C** and turn right. This old route is now worn to the

The monument to Sir Basil Grenville, killed in the battle of Lansdown Hill.

bedrock and exposed rock faces appear beside the track. Beyond the gate at the end of the lane continue straight on, with a view down to a little wooded valley, to arrive at a stone stile. Here the first of a new set of markers appears, in the form of metal standards, helping visitors negotiate the battlefield of Lansdown Hill. An information board gives details of the Civil War battle. Follow the path down towards the road, but before reaching it turn off to the right on the path dipping down through the trees, where the familiar beech are joined by no less impressive elm. The path then turns back up to reach the Grenville monument **50**. Replete with coats of arms and topped by a somewhat worn griffin, the monument commemorates Sir Bevil Grenville, who died in the battle.

Take the obvious grassy track away from the monument, cross over the road and go through a patch of rowan trees. Turn right on the minor road, and where that sweeps round to the left, go through the gate to take the roadside path towards the communications mast. Rejoin the road briefly by the mast and then take the narrow path between hedges. Once back in the open, the track works its way round the hill and an immense view opens out, dominated by the towers of Bristol but also including the Cotswold escarpment, snaking away to the north. On reaching the end of the promontory **D**, turn left through a gate by the trees and take the path heading sharply back down the opposite side of the headland. There are still fine views over wooded hillsides, but up ahead a line of conifers suggests a more artificial landscape, and sure enough they announce the arrival of the path at the edge of a golf course.

Look for a gate tucked away in the hedge and take the stony path, which turns to run alongside the course. Continue alongside the wood, and where that comes to an end turn right across the course and follow the track round, now with the course on the left. Continue on the broad track that swings away from the golf course, and just before reaching a stand of trees, turn left by a marker post **E** to head to the left towards a gate. The path remains more or less on the level as far as the end of the headland, then turns sharp left on to a broad path heading through farmland. The path goes through a wall with a ditch to the side – all that remains of an old hill fort, the last of the many met along the way. Turn right to follow the line of the wall, then continue round the edge of the field, emerging to pass the end of Bath racecourse **51**. Up ahead a tall folly tower can be seen: Beckford's Tower **52**. Nearly 130 feet (40 metres) high, it was built to give its owner a view of his house and the surrounding countryside. This section ends at Prospect Stile **F**, and there is indeed a topograph and a tremendous prospect out over the Avon valley and Bath – though, rather incongruously for a town famous for its Georgian architecture, the most prominent landmark is a giant gas-holder.

Once across the stile, take the obvious path, heading downhill. There is a little dog-leg, but the route continues on the

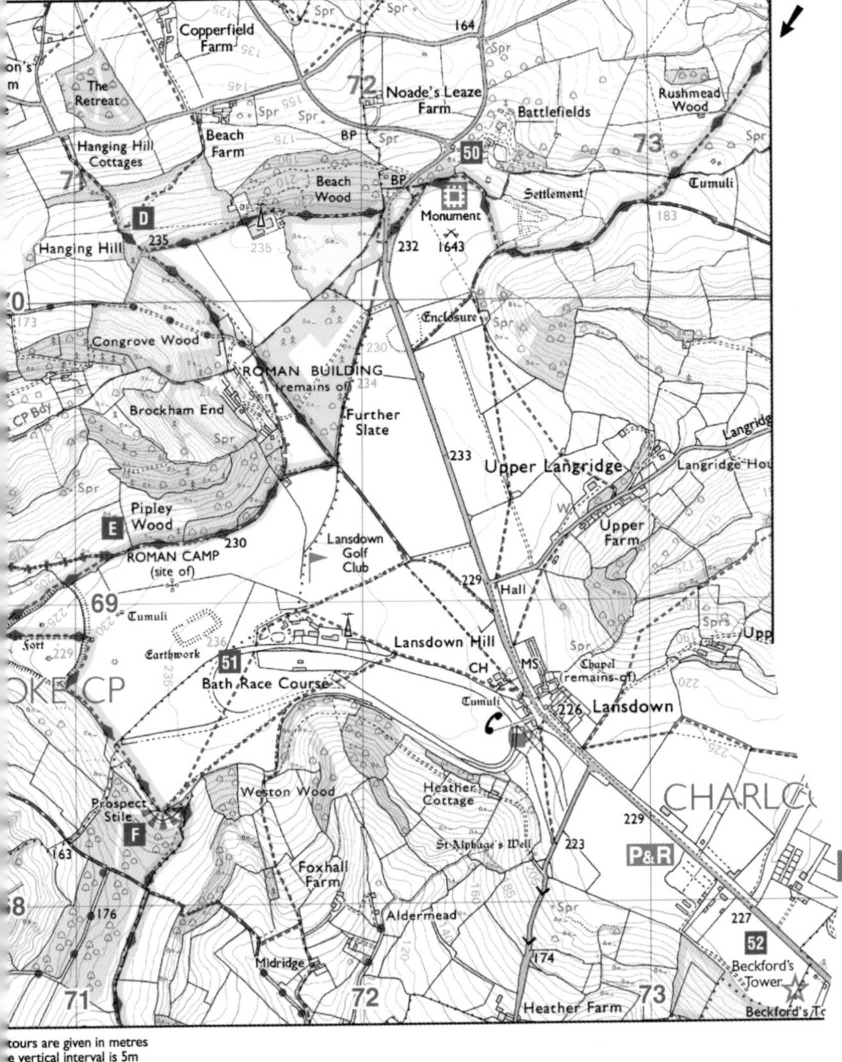

*The view from Prospect Stile, and seeing this panorama of the Avon valley it is easy to understand how this viewpoint got its name.*

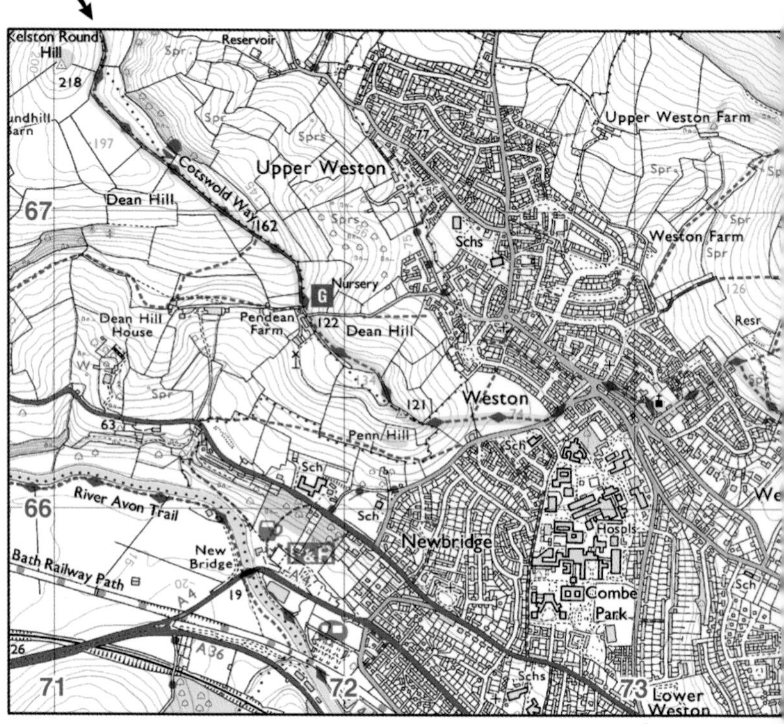


Contours are given in me
The vertical interval is

same obvious downhill route towards aptly named Round Hill. As it skirts the hill, the path swings round to the left to head towards the built-up area. Where the track joins the road by the houses **G**, keep going for a short way then turn right to take the path that traverses the grassy hillside, with another fine view of Beckford's Tower. The path swings left to head downhill past a prominent oak to reach a playing field. Head for the far right-hand corner to join the road in the Bath suburb of Weston. Turn left and go down Penn Hill Road, cross the main road by The Crown and Anchor, and go down Church Street, where the older houses give the first hint of delights to come. Having come all the way down to the valley, it is now time to climb back out again. Go past the church and continue to the left up Church Road, cross over the next road and take the footpath still heading relentlessly uphill. Go through the gate and turn right to the path beside the hedge to go briefly downhill. Leave the grassland by the little lane with a drystone wall on the right, cross the road and continue for what really is the last climb to emerge in a suburban enclave. A short walk brings the unmistakable architecture of rich stone and fine proportions for which Bath is famous.

Turn right **H** down Sion Hill, then take the footpath across High Common, with its golf course. Cross over the road into Victoria Park, with its inevitable Victoria monument, and turn left along Royal Avenue. Cross over the road, take a short left turn down Marlborough Lane, then take Gravel Walk – though no longer gravelled – which runs across the parkland in front of Royal Crescent **53**. This is one of the architectural showpieces of the city. Designed by John Wood the Younger in 1767, the elements are all very basic, but perfectly executed. The terrace swings in a graceful curve, the proportions of doors and windows are immaculate, monotony is avoided by breaking the façade with rows of Ionic columns, and the grassy park in front gives everyone space to stand back and admire. At the end of the walk, turn left, then right into Brock Street, which leads down to The Circus, built by John Wood the Elder in 1754. It has many of the qualities of Royal Crescent, but, as the name suggests, runs in a complete circle, and has rather more elaborate decoration, with different classical orders for the columns and pilasters at the different levels. Turn right into The Circus and leave down Gay Street to enter Queen Square. The route goes down Wood Street into Quiet Street, then right into New Bond Street to Burton Street and Union Street. Turn left through the Colonnade, passing the famous Roman Baths on your right, and turn right into Kingston Parade for the Abbey **54**, the official end to the Cotswold Way.

This is not the place to write a guide to the delights of Bath, which bring tourists from all round the world. Here you can visit Roman baths or their modern equivalent, stroll across the Avon on Pulteney Bridge, Bath's version of the Ponte Vecchio of Florence, wander among the streets or simply take a well-earned rest. Whatever the choice, no one could ask for a grander finale to a magnificent walk.

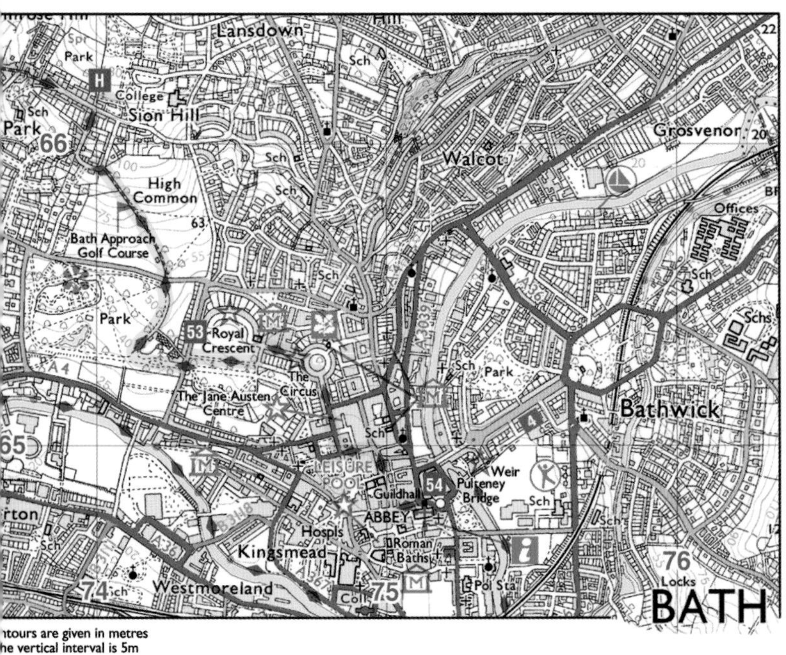


ntours are given in metres
he vertical interval is 5m

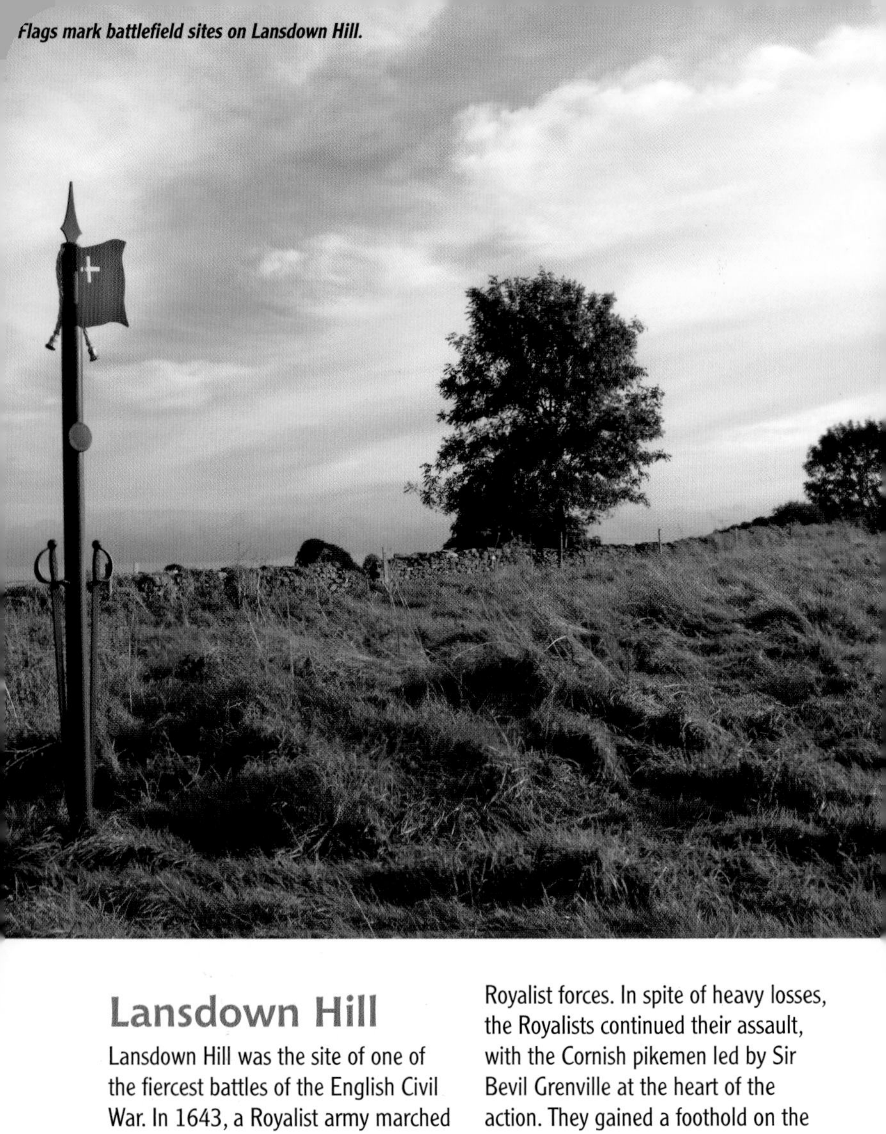

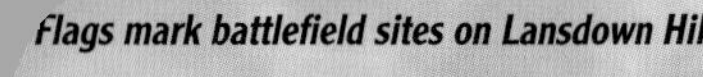

*Flags mark battlefield sites on Lansdown Hill.*

# Lansdown Hill

Lansdown Hill was the site of one of the fiercest battles of the English Civil War. In 1643, a Royalist army marched up from the south-west under the command of Sir Ralph Hopton and advanced on the key city of Bath. The task of defending the city fell to Sir William Waller, and he and his troops took up a defensive position on Lansdown Hill. They were heavily outnumbered, but they had the advantage of the high ground and were able to deploy their muskets and artillery to cause havoc among the Royalist forces. In spite of heavy losses, the Royalists continued their assault, with the Cornish pikemen led by Sir Bevil Grenville at the heart of the action. They gained a foothold on the plateau and the Parliamentarians retreated behind the wall that closes off the narrowest part of the headland. From there they continued to fire into the Royalist ranks. As night fell Waller, recognising that he was heavily outnumbered, retreated from the hill. It was at best a pyrrhic victory for Hopton, whose forces suffered far heavier casualties than those of the Parliamentarians.

# PART THREE
# Useful Information

## Planning your route

### Official Trail information

*The Cotswold Way National Trail* website (**www.nationaltrail.co.uk/cotswold**) has a wealth of information to help you plan your walk, including self-booked and organised accommodation, luggage carriers, route changes and public transport to and from the trail. A few useful sections include:

*Circular Walks:* For those who want just a taste of the Cotswold Way, or to dip their toes in before walking the whole route, a number of short, easy-to-follow circular walks are available to guide you smoothly along the National Trail in a series of bite-sized chunks. Each downloadable walk is designed to be as approachable and convenient as possible – whether you arrive by bus, car or on foot, they all benefit from the high quality standards followed by National Trails across the country.

*Friendship Trails:* The newest circular walk was developed as a 'friendship trail', twinned with the Jeju Olle walking route in South Korea to promote tourism and international cooperation between the two countries. Further twin trails are planned, including a partnership with the Bruce Trail in Canada.

*Hall of Fame:* If you walk the whole of the Cotswold Way, official certificates and badges to mark your achievement are available for free by joining the Cotswold Way Hall of Fame. It is also the best place to find out about other walkers' experiences along the trail.

*Disabled access:* The website also provides useful information for disabled visitors, including self-guided accessible circular routes and off-road mobility scooter hire.

*The Cotswold Way National Trail Companion* is also available to help you to plan your route, containing accommodation, local services, refreshments and other useful information – details about how to get hold of this can be found on the Cotswold Way website or by telephoning the Trail office.

### Other sources of information

A booklet *The Cotswold Way Handbook and Accommodation List* is published by The Ramblers' Association, Gloucestershire Area and is available from Tourist Information Centres. A film of The Cotswold Way, written and narrated by Anthony Burton, is available as a DVD or download from www.tvwalks.com.

## Transport

*Explore the Cotswolds by Public Transport* – a series of four free leaflets available from the *planning a trip* section of the Cotswold Way website. An introductory leaflet including access points, route plan and taster days out is backed up by three separate timetable guides which tell you all you need to know about getting to the National Trail without a car.

**Local and national coach, bus and rail information:**

Traveline ☎ 0870 6082608

ⓘ www.traveline.org.uk

*Countrygoer*, information on how to reach the local countryside:

ⓘ www.countrygoer.org.uk/cotswolds

**National Rail Enquiries:**

☎ 08457 484950

ⓘ www.nationalrail.co.uk

**Coach and bus information:**

National Express ☎ 08705 808078

ⓘ www.nationalexpress.com

# Tourist Information Centres

* Seasonal Opening Times

**Bath** Abbey Chambers, Abbey Church Yard, Bath BA1 1LY
☎ (UK callers) 0906 711 2000
(Overseas callers) +44(0) 844 847 5257
ⓘ www.visitbath.co.uk

* **Broadway** 1 Cotswold Court, Broadway WR12 7AA
☎ 01386 852937

**Cheltenham** 77 The Promenade, Cheltenham, GL50 1PJ
☎ 01242 522878
ⓘ www.visitcheltenham.gov.uk

**Chipping Campden** Old Police Station, High Street, Chipping Campden GL55 6HB
☎ 01386 841206
ⓘ www.campdenonline.org

**Chipping Sodbury** The Clock Tower, High Street, Chipping Sodbury BS37 6AH
☎ 01454 888686

**Gloucester** 28 Southgate Street, Gloucester GL1 2DP
☎ 01452 396572
ⓘ www.gloucester.gov.uk/tourism

**Stroud** The Subscription Rooms, George Street, Stroud GL5 1AE
☎ 01453 760960
ⓘ www.stroud.gov.uk

* **Winchcombe** The Town Hall, High Street, Winchcombe GL54 5LJ
☎ 01242 602925

* **Wotton-under-Edge** Heritage Centre, The Chipping, Wotton-under-Edge GL12 7AD
☎ 01453 521541
ⓘ www.wottonheritage.com

# Useful addresses

### Trail Management and Information

Cotswolds Conservation Board, Fosse Way, Northleach, Glos GL54 3JH
☎ 01451 862000
✉ cotswoldway@cotswolds aonb.org.uk
ⓘ www.nationaltrail.co.uk/cotswold

**Broadway**
Worcestershire County Council, Countryside Service, County Hall, Spetchley Road, Worcester WR5 2XG
☎ 01905 768214
✉ countryside@worcestershire.gov.uk
ⓘ www.worcestershire.gov.uk

**Hawkesbury to Cold Ashton** (plus parish of Bitton)
South Gloucestershire Council, Public Rights of Way, Elliot A1, Broad Lane, Yate BS37 7ES
☎ 01454 863646
✉ rightsofway@southglos.gov.uk
ⓘ www.southglos.gov.uk

**Cold Ashton to Bath** (excl. parish of Bitton)
Bath and North East Somerset Council, Public Rights of Way, Riverside, Temple Street, Keynsham BS31 1LA
☎ 01225 477532
✉ prow@bathnes.gov.uk
ⓘ www.bathnes.gov.uk

### Other contacts

Butterfly Conservation
ⓘ www.gloucestershire-butterflies.org.uk

English Heritage, South West: 29 Queen Square, Bristol BS1 4ND
☎ 0117 9750700
ⓘ www.english-heritage.org.uk

National Trust, Head Office, Heelis, Kemble Drive, Swindon, Wiltshire SN2 2NA
☎ 01793 817400
ⓘ www.nationaltrust.org.uk

Wessex: Eastleigh Court, Bishopstrow, Warminster, Wiltshire BA12 9HW
☎ 01985 843600

Natural England Head Office, 1 East Parade, Sheffield S1 2ET
☎ 0300 060 6000
ⓘ www.naturalengland.org.uk

Ordnance Survey, Adanac Drive, Southampton SO16 0AS
☎ 08456 050505
ⓘ www.ordnancesurvey.co.uk

Ramblers' Association, 2nd Floor, Camelford House, 87–90 Albert Embankment, London SE1 7TW
☎ 020 7339 8500
ⓘ www.ramblers.org.uk

Weathercall (Meteorological Office 5-day forecast) Wilts, Glos, Somerset
☎ 09068 405415
ⓘ www.weathercall.co.uk

Woodland Trust, Kempton Way, Grantham, Lincs NG31 6LL
☎ 01476 581111
ⓘ www.woodlandtrust.org.uk

## Places to visit on or near the Cotswold Way

(▲ = off route)

Broadway Tower Country Park
▲ Snowshill Manor (National Trust)
Stanway House and Fountain
▲ Gloucestershire & Warwickshire Steam Railway, Toddington Station
Hailes Abbey (English Heritage)
Winchcombe:
  Railway Museum, 23 Gloucester Street
  Folk and Police Museum, Old Town Hall
  Sudeley Castle and Gardens
Belas Knap long barrow (English Heritage)
▲ The Bird Park, Prinknash
Crickley Hill Country Park (National Trust/Gloucestershire County Council)
Coopers Hill Nature Reserve (Gloucestershire County Council)
Buckholt Wood – Cotswolds Commons and Beechwoods National Nature Reserve (Natural England)
▲ Painswick Rococo Gardens
▲ Stroud Museum in the Park
▲ Nailsworth, Dunkirk Mill, Gigg Mill
▲ Woodchester Park (National Trust) and Woodchester Mansion (Woodchester Mansion Trust)
Nympsfield long barrow (English Heritage)
▲ Uley long barrow (Hetty Pegler's Tump) (English Heritage)
▲ Owlpen Manor, Uley
Dursley Heritage Centre
Tyndale Monument
▲ Newark Park (National Trust)
Wotton-under-Edge Heritage Museum
Horton Court (National Trust)
Dyrham Park (National Trust)
Lansdown Battlefield Site
Bath:
  Postal Museum
  Museum of Bath at Work
  Herschel Museum of Astronomy
  Holburne Museum of Art
  Jane Austen Centre
  No. 1 Royal Crescent
  Roman Baths and Pump Room
  Building of Bath Museum
  Prior Park Landscape Garden (National Trust)
  The Fashion Museum
  Victoria Art Gallery

## Ordnance Survey Maps covering the Cotswold Way

Landranger (1:50,000) 150, 151, 162, 163, 172
Explorer (1:25,000) OL45, 155, 167, 168, 179

# The Official Guides to all o

ISBN 978 1 84513 785 4

ISBN 978 1 84513 781 6

ISBN 978 1 84513 718 2

ISBN 978 1 84513 643 7

ISBN 978 1 84513 602 4

ISBN 978 1 84513 565 2

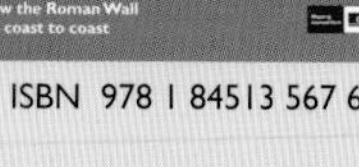

ISBN 978 1 84513 567 6

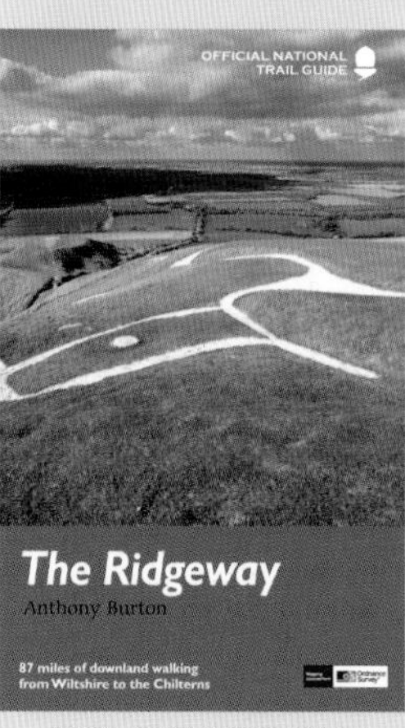

ISBN 978 1 84513 638 3

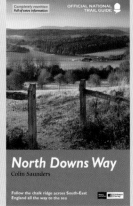


ISBN 978 1 84513 677 2

# Britain's National Trails

**Thames Path**

**Thames Path**

513 706 9

**Peddars Way and Norfolk Coast Path**

Bruce Robinson

90 miles from Breckland to salt marsh and sea cliffs

ISBN 978 1 84513 784 7

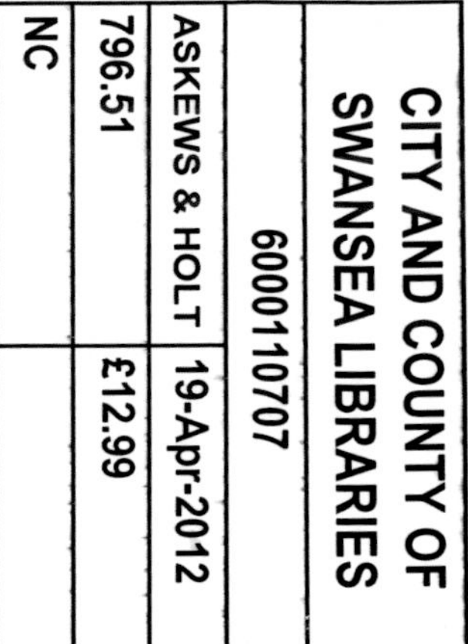


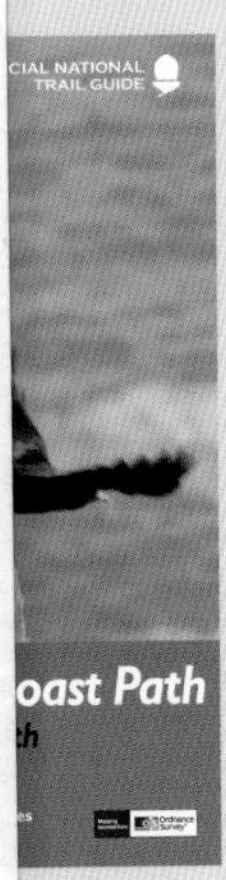

**oast Path**

513 641 3

**Offa's Dyke Path**

*SOUTH: Chepstow to Knighton*

Ernie and Kathy Kay and Mark Richards

Follow the ancient earthwork up the Wye Valley and alongside the Black Mountains

ISBN 978 1 84513 561 4

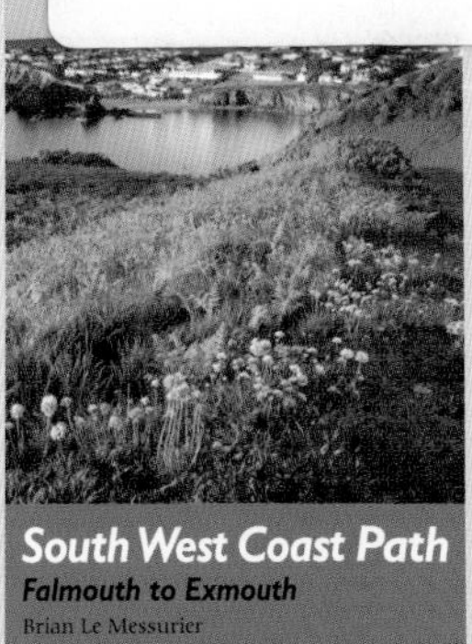

**South West Coast Path**

*Falmouth to Exmouth*

Brian Le Messurier

172 miles of dramatic coves, cliffs and beaches from Cornwall to Devon

ISBN 978 1 84513 564 5

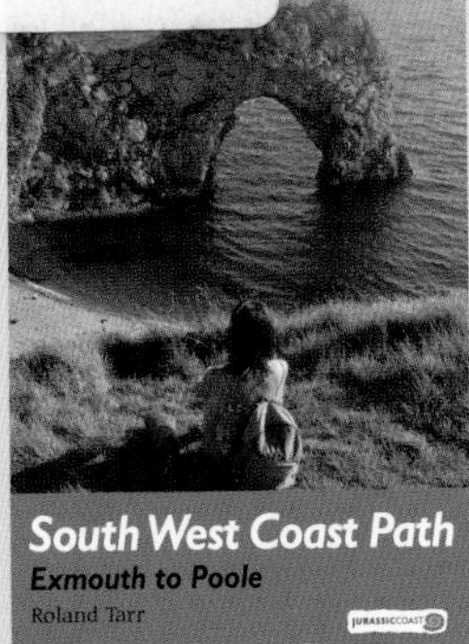


**South West Coast Path**

*Exmouth to Poole*

Roland Tarr

From Jane Austen's Cobb to Lulworth Cove – over 100 miles of historic coastline

ISBN 978 1 84513 642 0

ISBN 978 1 84513 312 2

ISBN 1 85410 957 X

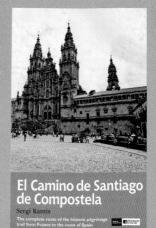

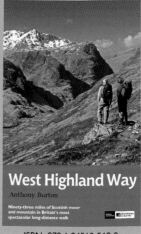